Also by Michael Crichton

Electronic Life

ELECTRONIC LIFE How to Think About Computers

Michael Crichton

Alfred A. Knopf   New York   1983

THIS IS A BORZOI BOOK
PUBLISHED BY ALFRED A. KNOPF, INC.

Grateful acknowledgment is made to the following for permission to reprint from previously published material:

Alfred A. Knopf, Inc.: Excerpts from *Tao Te Ching*, by Lao Tsu, translated by Gia-fu Feng and Jane English. Copyright © 1972 by Alfred A. Knopf, Inc. Used by permission of Alfred A. Knopf, Inc.

W. H. Freeman and Company: Short excerpt from Weizenbaum, *Computer Power and Human Reason*, which originally appeared in *Computer Models of Thought and Language* by Roger C. Schank and K. M. Colby, eds. Copyright © 1975 by W. H. Freeman and Company. All rights reserved.

Library of Congress Cataloging in Publication Data

Crichton, Michael, [*date*]   Electronic life.

Bibliography: p.
1. Microcomputers. I. Title.
QA76.5.C74   1983   001.64   83–48022
ISBN 0–394–53406–9

Manufactured in the United States of America

FIRST EDITION

To my parents

CONTENTS

ACKNOWLEDGMENTS

Twenty years ago, my first experience with computers occurred while I was a student of William Howells at Harvard. Because Howells treated these machines with good sense and good humor, I did, too. Howells regarded computers as a useful, sometimes exasperating tool, but he felt that to indulge fears about them was a waste of time. I can trace nearly all the attitudes expressed in this book to his own remarkably prescient views.

More recently, with the advent of small machines, many others have assisted me. Paul Bass, David Shire, Jim Leitzke, Stacy Keach, Andrew Grove, Ron Frankel, Clay Serbin, and Stephen Warady all helped me in innumerable ways.

I'd never have written a book had not Jack Roberts invited me to attend the International Design Conference in Aspen in June 1982. Jerry Lettvin was there; he proposed I write on this subject. Informal talks with other conference participants greatly influenced the shape of the text.

While preparing manuscript drafts, I received valuable suggestions from Caroline Ray, Lisa Faversham, Mike Rachmil, Kurt Villadsen, and Suzanne Crichton. Several of the people already mentioned read various drafts as well. Joseph Esherick translated the "I Ching" hexagram names. Bob Gottleib pulled the manuscript together with his usual apparent effortlessness.

Joseph Weizenbaum, Jerry Lettvin, Gloria Minsky, and Marvin Minsky reviewed the manuscript in its final stages and suggested important clarifications and additions.

I'm very grateful for all this help; whatever errors remain in the text are my own.

1

Electronic Life

This is a book about people and computers. It proceeds from several fundamental assumptions:

1. People are more important than computers.
2. Much of what we believe about computers is wrong.
3. It is easy to use a computer.
4. This is fortunate, because everybody's going to have to learn.
5. It is not so easy to use a computer wisely.
6. This is unfortunate, because everybody's going to have to learn.
7. Computers can actually be a lot of fun.
8. There are people who want to put a stop to that.

The proliferation of computers in recent years has been truly phenomenal. In 1978, there were about 5,000 desk-top computers in the United States. In 1982, there were 5 million. In 1980, there were 350,000 computer terminals communicating with a large machine elsewhere; by 1982, there were 3 million such terminals. By 1990, it is estimated there will be 80 million desk-top computers in the United States. By then, if you count microprocessors in weapon systems and home appliances, there will be a *billion* computers throughout the world. These small, cheap powerful devices will be everywhere, and they will have altered every aspect of human life, from the way we run our societies to the way we run our personal lives.

This may not be welcome news.

Industrial societies in the twentieth century have already undergone several revolutions in life-style as a result of new technologies, but these revolutions are now clearly perceived as mixed blessings. Even the most exhilarating single moment of twentieth-century technology—landing a man on the moon—is now perceived for what it was, the first giant step in the systematic militarization of space. And the nuclear power controversy in the United States is only comprehensible as a debate over whether our society should move in the direction of more technology or not. At the moment, our disaffection with technology seems to be so complete that even environmentalists prefer acid rain to nuclear waste.*

But in our disillusionment, it's worth remembering that the virtues of the technological future have been consistently oversold —often by the technologists, always by the press, and frequently by consumers themselves. Technology hype has been a feature of Western life for more than a century. But the technology doesn't create its own hype. We do it to ourselves, and if we're now disappointed or feel we've made wrong choices, we have only ourselves to blame.

Second, there are plenty of places left in the world where one can live a nineteenth-century life, an eighteenth-century life, or even a tenth-century life—but few people rush to live in them. Even the most disillusioned offspring of industrial society gets a rude shock on learning what the pre-technological world is *really* like.

The fact that industrial technology has been transformed from a problem-solving panacea to a problem-in-itself reveals more about us than it does about technology. If we are now inclined to

---

*Assuming that 1) our society won't cut power consumption dramatically; 2) alternative non-polluting power sources are not available today, although they will be in ten or twenty years; 3) we must therefore arrange for a temporary source of additional power; 4) neither coal nor nuclear power is an agreeable power alternative; 5) but we must choose one or the other, selecting the lesser of two admitted evils.

Assuming you're still with me, then the only decision is which is the lesser evil. Nuclear power is the lesser evil, if you can look at it rationally—which by now almost nobody can. (Trees didn't get to vote.)

view technology as a mixture of good and bad, advantage and disadvantage, cost and benefit, it simply means that we have adopted a more mature view. We've grown up a little.

Taking responsibility for choices is especially important when we think about computers, because computers are going to be in everyone's hands—like handguns. This makes computers a rather different kind of technology.

In contrast, consider automobiles. The technology of personal transportation doesn't allow the individual much freedom. You can't make your own automobile; design and manufacture are controlled by large corporations. You can't use an automobile without a road; road construction is controlled by governments. With an automobile your effective choices boil down to trivial matters such as cosmetic styling and accessories.

Similarly, mass-communications technology is out of your control. You can't easily create your own newspaper or television program; as an individual, you are effectively limited to complaining about large corporations that do.

And in many other areas of technology, we as individuals have come to recognize that we are powerless to control or shape the way technology is used. Like children with seemingly omnipotent parents, we must do as we are told. We are outsiders, resigned to that role. We can snipe at technology, but we can't really do anything about it.

But this is not true of computers. Small computers should not be perceived as just one more home appliance like a television set or a radio. Televisions and radios are passive receivers. A computer can function as both transmitter and receiver of information. Especially when connected to other computers, it places considerable technological power in individual hands.

There are several potential dangers in this situation, but the most fundamental is that people will not recognize the power they have. They may continue to behave as if computers were yet another form of technology controlled by "them"—the powerful faceless corporations and government institutions. If that happens, a great opportunity will have been missed—and a great responsibility shrugged off.

．．．

I'm always amazed at the number of people who fire off flashbulbs when photographing a sunset. If you ask them why they do it, they say, "Because it's getting dark, and when it's dark you need flash." These two statements are correct. At sunset, general illumination is decreased, and flash adds light when it is dark.

Unfortunately, flash has no appreciable effect beyond ten feet. The sun is some 50 billion miles away, or about 500 trillion times too far to be reached by a flashbulb. And in any case, sunlight provides an adequate exposure long after the sun itself has set.

In short, flash isn't necessary—and it doesn't do any good. Why are they firing off their flashbulbs? Because they have started with some correct information, and followed it to an absurd conclusion.

In this example, the outcome is harmless enough. But it reflects a substantial misunderstanding of the appropriate use of a camera. And it will give you a bad picture.

If you act according to a similar misunderstanding of the appropriate use of computers, the outcome may not be so harmless. Computers are powerful instruments that can be powerfully wrong when used wrongly.

Critics such as Joseph Weizenbaum fear that people will invest the computer with more authority than it deserves. In his book *Computer Power and Human Reason,* he raises serious issues about the impact of the computer on the unsuspecting and naïve user. Without doubt, inappropriate faith in the computer is an issue that must be faced.

But it seems to me that people will be able to see past the machine to the creator. Recognition of authorship occurs in apparently impersonal creations. For example, arcade games are increasingly advertised as the creation of one or another programmer.

I suspect the problem is self-limiting—both aroused and resolved by the machines themselves. If you fool around with a microcomputer for a while, you will get a sense of the subtleties that mechanical processes can produce. It is that sense, more than anything else, that one needs to face a newly "computerized" world with human balance and human judgment.

Most of this cheap, miniaturized computer power comes from industries in the Santa Clara Valley in northern California. The area is so dense with computer firms that it's often called Silicon Valley. And because the business of making computers and components is so fiercely competitive, some call it Silicon Gulch.

The firms in Silicon Gulch are revolutionizing every aspect of our lives—a fact that by now they know perfectly well. You might think that the source of all this change would be the source of ideas about what it means as well. But in true American fashion, Silicon Gulch firms are out to make money, not revolutions.

Consider miniaturization. You might imagine that somebody had a vision of all these tiny, powerful computers on desks around the world, and set out to make it happen. Not so: Andrew Grove, president of Intel Corporation, points out that miniaturization is a by-product of the attempt to make cheap computing power, and not a goal in itself.

The unit of fabrication is not the individual microchip, but a round wafer of silicon about three inches in diameter. Each wafer must be etched and treated in complex ways in a process that requires several days. Therefore, the more chips you can pack onto a single wafer, the cheaper each chip will be when you finally cut the wafer up into individual chips. If you can cram 250 chips on a wafer, they'll each be cheaper than a wafer that contains only 25 chips.

Similarly, if you can cram more components into each individual chip, then the cost of computing power will be cheaper.

This mundane business truth drives the mania for miniaturization. And the fact that miniaturization is a major factor in the widespread use of microprocessors is a kind of historical accident.

Nobody really sat down and planned it that way.

Of course, plenty of firms in Silicon Gulch make whole computers, not components, and they're focused directly on how these machines will be used, and by whom. However, Apple Computer, which really created the personal computer market, began as a garage business. The Apple was originally intended for games; the machine's inventors supposed they might sell a total of 20,000 units over a period of years. But most Apples are now used for business, and they sell at the rate of 25,000 a month.

So nobody really sat down and planned that either.

In 1979, Nolan Bushnell left Atari, having sold it to Warner Communications for $28 million. Within a year, video games had become so popular that Atari registered more than a billion dollars in sales; by 1982, the company was making back its selling price every two days.

Hard to imagine that was planned either.

The point of these stories is that nobody's in charge of the revolution. The suppliers of equipment and services have no better idea than you and I what's going on out there. It's a society-wide phenomenon.

In a sense, such an event is particularly likely to happen with computers, since the machines have no pre-determined function. For that matter, neither do computer programs. One reason why creating programs is so difficult is that after the program is written and put out into the marketplace, individual users take it and apply it to all sorts of tasks the authors never imagined. Naturally they sometimes get into trouble—and start calling the authors to complain, or to ask for help. Throughout the history of computers, the manufacturers of machines and programs have faced an almost impossible task in trying to anticipate use.

The history of the telephone provides an instructive example of what happens as a technology becomes widespread. Anyone over the age of fifty can probably remember when telephones had no dials. To make a call, you picked up the receiver and waited until an operator came on the line. You told the operator the number you wanted, and the call was placed for you. If you placed a long-distance call to some other city—a very exotic undertaking —you'd hear the operators talking to each other in their regional accents, arranging to route your call through their individual switchboards.

By the 1940s, this charming system was breaking down. There simply weren't enough operators to work the switchboards. In fact, projections of future telephone growth suggested that there weren't enough women in America—even if they all became telephone operators—to make the system run.

The solution was direct-dial telephones, which demanded all sorts of automatic switching devices and complex thingamajigs. This flashy new technology obscured a basic truth. The telephone company had actually solved the problem of insufficient operators by making everyone into his own operator. The number of telephone operators now equaled the telephone-using population.

For nearly everyone, the telephone provided the first experience of direct interaction with a computing machine. People had to learn the harsh rules of computer interaction: numbers only, and numbers presented in a specific order. The telephone responded to exactly what you dialed, whether you'd made an error or not. There was no friendly human voice to catch your mistakes.

After an initial period of grumbling, people discovered they preferred direct dialing. It was faster and it was totally private. The few situations where an operator was still required, such as for overseas calls, became irritating. The fact that you couldn't do the whole thing yourself was now perceived as a flaw, not a virtue.

Of course, in organizational hierarchies, telephone dialing acquired certain status connotations. Highly placed executives affected a total inability to dial for themselves, requiring their secretaries to do it for them. But virtually everyone understood this for what it was, a status ploy. No one in his right mind was really unable to dial a phone. Telephone dialing was an essential skill for everyday life.

And eventually the affectation fell away, as affectations do. A busy executive could place his own calls faster than a secretary could do it for him. And no one wanted to look as if he weren't busy.

Computers are now going through the same series of transformations. Everyone is becoming his own operator. Direct access means power; and it's becoming a necessary skill for everyday life.

But the analogy can be extended further. Just as the telephone doesn't care where you are calling, the computer doesn't care what use you make of it. And just as the telephone company has had to go to great lengths to devise a simple direct-dial system anywhere in the world, computer programmers have gone to great lengths to devise methods that allow you to create your own programs.

Computer languages were the first step, but that's far from satisfactory for many users, who don't want to know so much about the machine. The second step was to create programs that will write your programs for you. You answer a series of questions in regular English about what you want to happen, and then the machine itself writes the new program.

Many such "code generating" programs exist. Using them, you can set up the computer any way you like, without knowledge of computer language. In short, just as you have become your own telephone operator, you become your own programmer.

With home computers, this trend started with serious business programs for accounting and data management. But it has now extended through the full range of programming, even to games; programs exist to write other game programs, so you can sit down and design the sort of game you'd like to play, without bothering to learn machine language.

It's at this point that the question of who's running the revolution becomes answered. You are. Through a series of accidents, computers have become small, cheap, and widespread. Because users employ computers for everything under the sun, programmers are being forced to create general tools to allow you to do your own programming.

These two events put you firmly in charge. You're a general, not a private. In fact, there are no privates. Step to the mirror and salute yourself—then go carry out your own orders.

This book began as practical notes for friends who had just bought home computers, and were now staring with horror at their new acquisitions. I would help them get started and leave a set of these notes for reference. Because my notes were written on a word processor, I added a little more each time. I began to get feedback.

You should have mentioned this or that, they'd tell me. The notes got longer and longer.

I began to realize that first-time computer users needed help with something not covered in most books and manuals—namely, an attitude to take toward this new kind of machine. How to think about computers, not just how to use them.

Meanwhile, I had started to develop computer programs for film production, a business that previously used no computers at all. I was plunged into a whole new world: buying minicomputer hardware, supervising programmers, and trying to convince suspicious specialists that their lives would be simpler and better (and they would not lose their jobs) if they used these machines. The new programs were easy to use, but visitors became so anxious around a computer terminal they literally couldn't recognize that they could save millions of dollars using them.

Again I was thrown back to attitudes.

In June, 1982, I attended the International Design Conference in Aspen, Colorado, and watched professionals in another field struggling with computers and what they meant. Once again, attitudes seemed critical.

Computers really are unprecedented machines in everyday life, and they do demand a whole set of new attitudes. This leaves people feeling helpless and lost.

I hope this book helps. At the very least, having written it, I can stop talking about it myself.

Because I feel that attitudes toward computers are initially more important than facts, this is a book of my opinions—or, if you prefer, my prejudices. I'm not judicious or fair; I'm telling you how I think about small computers. Other computer users may disagree. If you do, write your own book.

Second, the book is simplified, and any simplification risks inaccuracy. But I don't think beginners need fret over such details as why the IBM PC isn't a true 16-bit computer; they can pick that up later. You have to start somewhere, and most texts start at too advanced a point.

Third, this book is practical, even in its speculative discussions. You can get lost in the theoretical aspects of computer art, or artificial intelligence. If you want to do so, this book won't help.

Fourth, I'm fussy about language, because language creates a structure for thinking—which is the subject of this book. Language suggests possibilities and limits, often unconsciously. I've watched beginners struggle repeatedly with terminology. The language of computers has drifted and shifted with thirty years of technological change. Indistinct words, like out-of-focus snapshots, should be discarded. I also feel certain ways of speaking should be avoided, because they imply the computer is doing something it really isn't.

Finally, this book focuses on microcomputers and minicomputers—small machines that cost from a few hundred to several thousand dollars. If you're interested in large mainframe computers, most of what I say won't be useful.

2

Practical Matters A to Z

Afraid of Computers

Everybody is.

The computer is a new machine. It requires new skills, new orientation, new ideas. It's changing our lives. Nobody in his right mind likes that.

Although we've all been fed a load of psychological pap that says learning is fun and challenges are exciting, human beings are inherently conservative. Change means stress. Change makes us uncomfortable and fearful.*

Watch people learning to drive a car. Do they appear to be having fun? Of course not. They're terrified—and dangerous besides. Watch people learning to play the piano. Are they having an exciting, challenging time? No. They're mastering feelings of frustration and boredom, trying to hit the damn keys right.

There's a fundamental truth here: human beings don't like change.

We're also told children accept change more readily than adults. If so, why must parents drag their child kicking and screaming to a new school, a new dance or music class? Why is divorce so hard on children? Why do children always oppose a change of residence?

Children tolerate change no better than adults. It's simply

---

*Don't confuse change with newness. Newness is pleasant. You probably genuinely enjoy a new car or new clothes, but these new items are not really different from the ones they replace. As a matter of fact, automobile and clothing designers are careful to create the appearance of change without actually changing much—because they know people don't like genuine change.

more acceptable for them to resist openly—and in the end, they know they have grown-ups to soothe them and help them adjust to new things.

Since it's considered poor form for an adult to kick and scream, adults learn to reject change by more subtle mechanisms. These mechanisms protect the adult from admitting fear, but they are not healthy because they interfere with learning.

So whoever told you that you're supposed to enjoy new things is wrong. You're perfectly justified in hating new things and finding them frustrating. A certain amount of kicking and screaming is useful.

Fear of computers is normal.

But it is not helpful. People who fear computers cannot use them wisely. Either they reject the machines out of hand, and are deprived of the legitimate benefits of computers, or they accept the machines but remain so intimidated that whatever flashes up on a screen is taken as received truth. You can get into trouble either way.

Read on.

Anatomy, Computer

Faced with an unfamiliar computer, experienced programmers do an interesting thing.

They do nothing.

They stand and look at the machine. After a moment, they may make some simple observation like "Hmmm, it's got a hard disk drive," or "I see it's got a built-in printer."

What they're doing is checking out the anatomy of the machine—finding where things are. This is a logical first step before trying to operate the machine.

Beginners skip this step. Either they throw up their hands in horror and announce that computers are beyond them or they plop down at the keyboard and say, "Okay, what do I do?"

What you do first is nothing. Whether you're in a store or a home or an office, first step back and look. Take your time.

You will probably be looking at a collection of off-white boxes. Your first task is to determine which box contains the *computer* itself.

Do this by finding the *keyboard.* The computer is either built into the keyboard box (Apple II, Atari, VIC) or directly attached to it by a cable (IBM, Epson, DEC). Once you've identified where the computer is, you can stop worrying about it for now, and maybe forever.

Meanwhile, the keyboard may have upset you because it has more keys than a typewriter. Don't fret over the extra keys. A computer keyboard is basically a typewriter keyboard, no matter how many keys it has. (And in time you'll learn that the extra keys make things easier, not harder.)

Now find the *disk drives.* These are boxes with little slots. They may be separate, or built into the computer itself. Either way they work the same. Disk drives store information for the computer.

Even if disk drives are new to you, they're not difficult. Each drive has a little slot with a little latch. The drives take floppy disks of black plastic; you probably see some lying around nearby. Hold a disk with your thumb over the label and slide it into the slot. Close the latch. Open the latch and take the disk out. So much for disk drives.

Next find the *monitor.* It may be a TV set, or it may just look like one. In any case, it works like a TV. It's got an on/off switch, brightness and contrast controls. No big deal.

Now find the *printer.* The printer is just an electric typewriter without a keyboard.

Having located the computer, keyboard, disk drives, monitor, and printer, you've identified the essential components of the system. This is all you need to deal with at the moment.

But there may be additional things lying around. There may be a *modem,* to link the computer to a telephone line. There may be *game paddles* or a *joystick* for playing games. There may be a *graphics tablet* for drawing pictures. Don't worry about any of this extra equipment now. Notice it exists, and ignore it.

Sit down and focus on the main computer components. You may want to label each component with a 3″ × 5″ card. But however you go about it, take the time to get the basic anatomy —computer, keyboard, disk drives, monitor, printer—clear in your mind.

The reason for emphasizing this spatial orientation is that a computer is a system of component parts, like a component stereo.

If you own a stereo, you probably have no idea how it actually works, and couldn't care less—but you know what each box does. If you didn't understand stereo components, you might try to tune in a radio station by twirling the knobs on your tape deck (which will get you nowhere).

Yet many beginning computer users struggle for hours through similar sorts of errors, just because they never took the time to figure out what each component does.

The minimum information you need to run a computer system is the functions of the different components.

To continue the stereo analogy, you can think of the computer as the amplifier.

The amplifier just makes music louder. It doesn't care what the music is. Yet by itself the amplifier is silent. You have to provide it with a source of music—either prerecorded records or tapes, or live signals from a radio. In addition, you have to provide the amplifier with an output device, such as speakers or headphones. Without them, the amplifier will remain silent.

Similarly, the computer is silent without a source of information, from prerecorded floppy disks or from keyboard input. And the computer also needs an output device, in this case a monitor or a printer, so you will know what is happening.

Thus a component stereo and a component computer are quite close in functions. Here's the analogy in summary:

Stereo	*Computer*

INPUT DEVICES

| Tape Deck, Phonograph | Disk Drive |
| Tuner | Keyboard |

PROCESSING DEVICES

| Amplifier | Computer |

OUTPUT DEVICES

| Speakers, Headphones | Screen, Printer |

RECORDING DEVICES

| Tape Deck | Disk Drive |

All this is simple enough. But note one crucial distinction between a stereo and a computer: a computer has memory and a stereo does not. Because people are not accustomed to machines with memories, the computer memory is the most difficult thing to get a "feel" for.

Read on.

Applications

Everybody wants to know "Why should I get one? What good is it to me? What do I do with it?"

When they don't get a crisp answer—and they never do—they become discouraged.

But the problem lies in the question, not the answer. In a large cosmopolitan city, if someone asked you "What kind of food is available here?" you'd probably answer that there are all kinds of food, and that the person can find whatever he wants.

But this doesn't satisfy the questioner, who now asks, "Yes, but what kind of food am I hungry for?"

That's a foolish question, yet it's the question people are really asking about computers, and not getting an answer to. Nobody can tell you what you're hungry for. And nobody can tell you how to use a computer. You'll have to decide for yourself.

Nearly 3 million small computers were sold in 1982, so a lot of people had some application in mind. It may help to know how other people use their computers. There are four main areas of use:

Business. Fifty-four percent of small machines are devoted to business applications, where they do accounting, bookkeeping, inventory, and financial planning.

Personal/Home Management. People balance their checkbooks, plan the family budget, keep track of recipes, and do word processing for personal letters.

Education. Programs are available to teach a great range of skills interactively; people learn quickly and easily this way. Word processing is valuable to older students, who frequently use a computer for nothing else.

Entertainment. The computer is the best toy in human history. Many people buy them to use as a toy, although few will admit it.

But all this may still not help you decide what you're hungry for. In that case, consider Bertie's Butler.

Bertie's Butler: Version I

Your rich Uncle Bertie in England dies, and bequeaths you his butler. Pretty soon the butler arrives on the doorstep of your house or apartment.

What in God's name are you going to do with a *butler?*

Your life worked perfectly fine without him. You don't have any use for a butler. I mean, you can't see him dressing you or serving dinner or doing those regular butler chores, as if you were Cosmo Topper.

Furthermore, although he's friendly enough, he doesn't know America, so you have to explain every little detail to him. If you ask him to go to the post office for you, you first need to tell him where the post office is, and how much stamps cost, and—oh, he's just more trouble than he's worth, this butler. And his standing around makes you nervous.

You do the sensible thing: you try to get rid of him.

But he won't leave.

He explains that according to Uncle Bertie's will, his expenses are fully paid, and he's your butler for life. You're stuck with him.

You resign yourself to having this butler hanging around forever. But as time goes by, you begin to notice certain advantages. Trivial advantages, but agreeable. It's nice that the house is always watched. It's nice that there's someone to accept UPS packages and answer the phone when you're at work. You're freed from these petty things. And it's nice that there's always someone to play chess with you on spare evenings.

As the butler proves his reliability, you let him take care of some of your bills, type your letters, do a little shopping. He starts to remind you of things, like your mother's upcoming birthday. He's very good with the kids; they love him.

After a year, you can't imagine life without your butler. It's not that he does anything really vital; it's just that he's so helpful in a dozen little ways. You realize you were a fool to try to get rid of him. In fact, now you wish you had two butlers. . . .

Bertie's Butler: Version II

Your rich Uncle Bertie in England dies, and bequeaths you his butler. You're delighted! You can't wait for this wonderful servant to arrive and change your life! Eventually the butler arrives on the doorstep of your house or apartment.

Immediately you notice he is in formal dress with a stiff white collar. This is not your thing at all—you imagined a more casual servant. Nevertheless you set him to work. And right away you discover problems.

For one thing, the butler speaks British, not American. Your car has a punctured tire so you ask him to "fix the flat." You return home to find he's redecorated the apartment and ignored the car.

Furthermore he doesn't know America, so you have to explain every little detail to him. If you ask him to go to the post office for you, you first must tell him where the post office is, and how much stamps cost, and the American currency system, and—oh, he's much more trouble than doing the job yourself.

He's friendly enough but he's rather stubborn. He does things his way. It becomes clear that if you're going to use him, you'll have to change. But you don't want to change.

You resign yourself to having this useless butler hanging around. After a year, you can't imagine why you wanted him in the first place. It's not that he's so bad; it's just that he never does anything without patient directions from you. He's a waste of time, this butler. . . .

Somewhere between these two stories lies most people's experience of a computer invading their lives. The lessons are clear. First, the computer is an interactive device. It will do as much as you teach it to do. But teaching it takes time—your time. And second, don't expect too much from any computer.

It's just a machine.

Bunny Slopes and Instamatics

If you're learning to ski, start on the bunny slopes. They're not terribly exciting, but you can learn on them comfortably and you won't get hurt. You'll be reassured by the other beginners, who, like you, are also falling down a lot.

But in every ski lodge, you find certain advanced skiers who subtly make you feel you're not really skiing unless you're going a hundred miles an hour down sheer ice.

The fact that these experts need to put you down is their problem. It's more fun to learn in a learner's environment.

In the same way, start with a beginner's equipment. If you're taking your first photos, an Instamatic will be perfectly adequate. You can get Instamatic film everywhere; passing strangers on the street know how to operate it; it's simple to use. You're free to concentrate on the real purpose of a camera, which is to take pictures.

The person who reminds you that the Instamatic is a pretty lousy camera isn't helping you. He may tell you a Nikon is a snap to use—but it isn't. It's tougher to load film into a Nikon than it is to use an Instamatic from start to finish.

You can always buy a better camera later, if you decide you want to get involved with f-stops and focal lengths and depth-of-field and film speed and all the other things that you must know to operate a complex camera.

If the equipment is too complicated or the slopes too steep, you won't have any fun and you will eventually stop trying.

The Apples and TRS-80s and Atari 800s of this world are computers designed for beginners. These machines exist in a bunny-slope environment: lots of other stumbling beginners around, lots of help available. If you're a novice, you will have an easier time, and more fun, starting with these machines.

Buying a Computer

It's harder to buy a computer than to use one.

This is literally true: the average buyer spends seven hours purchasing his machine, and anyone can learn to use a computer in much less time than that. To buy a computer, follow these rules:

1. *Buy from a store, not a mail-order house.* Mail-order prices are cheaper, but if you're reading this book, you need the support a store provides. A good store has salesmen who speak English; sells both machines and programs; does its own repairs; and either has its own classes or provides training and installation. The store should also be conveniently located, since you'll probably have to lug the machine back there at least once in the first year.

2. *Buy a program, not a machine.* This is the hardest rule to follow. When you walk into the store, you will see all these computers and glowing screens. Your consumer instincts lead you to focus immediately on the machines, their different designs, keyboards, screens, and so on. Resolutely ignore the machines. Turn your back on them, and talk to the salesman about what you want a computer to do.

You must decide the use for yourself—preferably before you come to the store. (See APPLICATIONS.) Perhaps you want to do word processing, and also to play games. Perhaps you want the machine for business accounting, but explicitly want no games because you don't want your employees wasting time playing them. (Forget that; they'll play games anyway.) Perhaps you want a machine for your family's exploration—and thus want a learning tool, or a toy.

These uses require programs, and only secondarily machines to run those programs. Once you've decided what programs you want, choosing a machine is much simpler.

3. *Buy a flexible machine.* As with Bertie's butler, you don't really know how you'll end up using the computer. But you can be pretty sure that once you have the machine working at its primary use, you'll want it to do more. You may not think you will, but you will.

Therefore the safest thing is to get a machine with lots of optional hardware, programs, attachments, and other stuff. To determine how flexible your machine is, ask these questions:

How many programs are available? If the machine you're considering doesn't have a fat book listing programs for sale, or if the salesman hands you a sheet printed by the computer manufacturer, think carefully about your purchase.

How many languages are available? The number of programming languages is a good indicator of how much programming has already been done on the machine, and how quickly future programs will be adapted to it. (See LANGUAGES, COMPUTER.)

How many operating systems will it run under? The operating system determines the number of available programs. Specifically, think carefully before you buy a machine that can't run under CP/M. (See OPERATING SYSTEM.)

How much hardware is available? Can you buy attachments to make the machine speak? Draw on a graphics tablet? Use a light pen or a "mouse"? How many different manufacturers sell hardware for your machine?

How many books are available? If there's a store in your town that specializes in computer books, visit it just to look at the number of books available for your machine as opposed to others. Find out how many magazines either are devoted to your machine or carry regular articles on your machine.

You may never want any of the books, magazines, hardware, or programs. But you can't be sure, and a limited machine costs as much as a flexible one. Keep your options open.

There is one situation in which you should not keep your options open. If you want a special-purpose machine for full-time use, buy a special-purpose machine. (See DEDICATED MACHINES.)

4. *Never buy a machine unless it does the job now.* The salesman may promise that a machine will have just the piece of hardware or exactly the program you want next month. But it may not come next month. It may not come for a year. It may not come ever.

This harsh fact has always been true of computers. In many respects, the history of an established, reputable company like IBM is a chronicle of salesmen managing to keep customers happy despite the fact that the machines arrive late and don't perform as promised. The computer business is ruthlessly competitive, and salesmen display excessive optimism to make a sale.

5. *Don't buy a brand-new machine or program.* Computers and programs are complex creations, and new ones have bugs—sometimes severe bugs. The Apple III computer was released

prematurely, and then withdrawn for a time because of its problems. A great many programs have been hastily released, and just as hastily "updated" as the manufacturers correct the bugs.

If you wouldn't buy a new-model car for at least a year, then you don't want to buy a new machine or program until it's been out and tested for a while either.

6. *Don't save money on monitors or printers.* Beginners often imagine monitors or printers are less important than the computer itself. They're not. Your experience of the computer is largely determined by how the type looks on the screen or on the printed page. Fuzzy type and blurry print are a drag.

It is much easier to add than to upgrade equipment. Unless the store allows you to try out a monitor or a printer, don't accept a cheap one. You'll soon wish you had something better, and you'll find nobody wants your cheap equipment any more than you do. (See MONITOR; PRINTER.)

7. *Make the salesman write down what you have bought.* Do it in detail at the time of purchase. (See CONFIGURATION.)

8. *Make the store set it up.* The store should either install the computer for you or assemble it in front of you at the store, showing you how it goes together. You should get some minimal instruction in using the machine.

9. *Don't test programs.* Many stores let you try out program packages on a trial basis. Beware this kindness: you can waste a lot of time trying out programs. It's faster to read reviews in magazines, or to ask other users. Even satisfied users know a program's limitations. If you must test, narrow your decision to two choices, and make the decision quickly at home.

10. *Don't buy a prepaid service contract.* Unless your machine is used only for business, and unless the contract stipulates the repairman will come the same day to your office, you don't need a service contract.

Byte

A computer is just a bunch of on/off switches. How does it use these switches to store information such as words, letters, and numbers? It does it exactly the way you'd do it if you were faced with the same problem.

Consider the following detective story:

There's a kidnapper at large. You've narrowed the suspects to four men: Andrew, Ben, Charlie, or Dave. You and the police set a trap for him. One of these four will come to your house tonight, while the police hide outside. Your job is to identify the kidnapper, signal his name to the police, and then keep him occupied while the police recover the child.

But how will you signal? You can't pick up the phone and call. Eventually, you and the police hit upon the clever idea of signaling the first letter of his name by casually switching on the house lights after he arrives. Since there are four possibilities, you will need two lights:

KIDNAPPER	LIVING ROOM LIGHT	BEDROOM LIGHT
Andrew	on	on
Ben	on	off
Charlie	off	on
Dave	off	off

Charlie walks through the door; you turn on the bedroom light; the police recover the child, and you're a hero.

Of course, if you had more suspects, you'd need more lights to signal. If you had twenty-six suspects, from Andrew to Zeke—in other words, all the letters of the alphabet—you'd end up needing six lights in various on/off combinations to signal.

It turns out that a computer also requires six on/off switches —or *bits*—to identify one letter of the alphabet. But the computer must deal with more than just the alphabet. It must handle numbers from zero to nine, punctuation marks, and many other symbols. A computer actually uses eight switches to store a single piece of information. With eight switches, a computer can handle any of 256 symbols.

Thus for a computer the unit of information storage is a group of eight switches working together. These eight bits are called a *byte.* One letter of the alphabet stored in the computer takes one byte.

The capacity of the computer to hold information is measured in bytes. This measurement is usually in thousands of bytes, or *kilobytes,* represented by the letter "K." A computer with the memory to store 64,000 bytes is referred to as a 64K computer.

Calvinists, Computer

One of the delights of any new technology is that it is, for a while, free. Government hasn't figured out how to regulate it; businessmen haven't figured out how to squeeze all the joy out of it; educators haven't figured out how to teach it into tedium. For a while, the new technology is in the hands of enthusiasts, with nobody to tell them what to do.

The early barnstorming days of manned flight created a fellow-feeling among enthusiasts that triumphed over the regimented horrors of World War I. The early days of movies, records, and television were each characterized by a period of glorious freedom and invention, followed by ever-increasing organization and decline. These technologies show a kind of inverted life span, with the Golden Years falling at the beginning, not the end.

Personal computers are only about six years old, and already the rule-makers and the dogmatists are out in force. They're the computer Calvinists. They are shocked by these goings-on. Look: do you mean to say that a person can buy a machine, take it home, teach himself programming, and then use the computer however he pleases? Without first being told the proper way? Without paying any attention to the rules? Everybody doing whatever he wants? That's anarchy! It can't be allowed to continue! Let's have some classes and some courseware and let's insist on computer literacy! By God, let's put a stop to this!

Of course, no Calvinist talks this way, even to himself. On the contrary, Calvinists tell you everything they're doing is for your own good.

Personally I hope that, for once in the twentieth century, a new technology will stay free. Because the rule-makers always manage to kill the essence while tidying up the details. Dogma replaces direct experience, and ritual becomes reality.

Right now, we are at the edge of a new era of unlimited potential. Nobody can see what is going to happen; nobody knows. There are no experts, and there's no reason slavishly to follow anybody's instructions about anything.

Including mine.

Do it your way, and have all the fun you can.

Compatible

At the start of any new technology, compatibility is a problem. When color television began, there were competing methods of transmission until one method predominated. In the early days of audiotapes, there were cassettes and eight-track cartridges, until eventually cassettes became the standard. There are now two non-compatible methods of home video recording, VHS and Beta-max, which seem for the moment to be coexisting.

Computer compatibility is a far more complex issue than any of these earlier examples. Right now, every computer is incompatible with every other computer; programs created for one brand will not run on another without modification.

This situation presents such obvious drawbacks that it can't continue forever—but it will probably continue for many years to come. In the meantime, a buyer must recognize that he is buying both a machine and access to a collection of programs. If you plan to wait until computer programs are as standardized as LP records, you'll wait a long time.

Computer

Originally, a person with a talent for calculation. In the eighteenth and nineteenth centuries, mathematical prodigies were referred to as computers.

During World War II, there was a desperate need for computers; whole roomfuls of people worked to draw up gunnery charts, or to perform the calculations for atomic research. An insufficient supply of human computers was the principal impetus behind developing mechanical devices to perform these functions.

Naturally enough, the first machines were also called computers, although they were really what we would now call calculators. They did mathematical computation exclusively, and had no other reason for being. The first inventors felt that four computers would be sufficient to carry out the world's computational work —after all, how much use was there for a computing machine?

After World War II, more advanced machines were developed with the ability to manipulate any kind of symbols—numbers, alphabetical letters, visual images, anything. These devices were still called computers, though they were applied to non-mathematical tasks such as language translation. At this time, the term "machine" became popular; it seemed more accurate to speak of "machine translation" rather than "computer translation" of a language, for example.

By the mid-1970s, it was clear that the future of these devices lay overwhelmingly in non-mathematical applications. Industrial societies were increasingly concerned with information processing, and the bulk of information took the form of images and text, not numbers. "Computer" is less and less appropriate for machines that do this work, although the word is clearly here to stay.

Computer Art

Computer art has been around for twenty years, and the term now has certain widespread assumptions attached to it. Most people have seen computer art, particularly computer graphics, which have been used in movies and television commercials extensively during the past ten years. As the products called "computer art" have become more familiar, it has become harder to ask whether they should be called computer art—or whether there is, really, such a thing as computer art.

Art has always been a human activity. Even when mechanical processes are involved, we have focused on the human aspects. Thus a machine-woven rug can be appreciated for its human design, while the perfection of the execution of that design is uninteresting since it is mechanical.

But the concept of computer art threatens to upset this traditional view, because the computer is not as elementary as a weaving machine. "Computer art" carries the suggestion that the computer may have created the work itself, and not merely acted as an agency for execution.

Although we never speak of paintbrush art or pencil art or typewriter art, we do speak of computer art as if it were something different.

Can the computer create something? At first glance it seems obvious that it can. Animated computer graphics, with their fluid transitions and whiplash perspectives, look strikingly new. And if one watches the machine doing animation work, there seem to be lengthy periods when the computer is acting "on its own."

But if one observes these processes in more detail, it becomes clear that creation is not occurring within the machine. First of all, computer graphics are not unique. Computers have yet to generate anything that cannot be done by hand—and usually already has been done. Second, the apparent ability of the computer to act "on its own" is the outcome of thousands of hours of patient human effort to refine its instructions. The computer can manipulate a shape for us if we have already informed it what a shape is, what the rules for shape manipulation are, what this specific shape is, and so forth.

You can start an automobile engine and it will run by itself, too, but that doesn't mean it's being creative. It's just running.

But what about the situations where the computer makes something not precisely determined by the programmers? I can write an indeterminate art program, such as the simple one in the appendices. The more general my commands, the more likely it is that I will get back something that surprises me. Is that surprise proof of creativity?

No, because I still had to give the computer a rather long list of instructions. Inescapably, I must tell it the boundaries within which it acts, and the rules of behavior within those boundaries. Because I do so, the essential creativity remains with me, not the machine.

If this argument leaves you with some nagging doubts, consider a simpler example. You build a clock. Any creativity in that step is clearly your own—the clock is just a mechanical device. Now you modify your clock so it rings every hour. This makes the clock more complex in its behavior, but it still cannot be said to have creativity. It's just doing what it's made to do. Now you add a variety of other effects—whistles, shrieks, smoke bombs, Bronx cheers—and you arrange for these effects to go off at random. Now neither you nor anyone else knows exactly how the clock will behave. It will appear quite complicated as it puffs and whistles and burps through the day. It may produce some unusual combinations of effects. But it never does anything truly creative, be-

cause it never goes beyond the limitations of its own structure—
a structure that you provided.

I have reached this conclusion sadly and reluctantly. I have been
a writer for nearly twenty years and I am lazy. When I first
brushed up against these machines, I immediately thought to put
them to work doing the hard job of making up stories. This did
not strike me as impossible, at least in simple ways.

After a famous mystery writer died, a cardboard wheel was
found pinned to the wall of his study. This wheel was marked like
wedges of a pie with notations such as "Get knocked out" or "Go
to another place." Apparently the writer spun the wheel whenever
he was stuck for a plot change. That's common enough; in *A
Moveable Feast,* Hemingway mentions incorporating apparently
chance events in writing. If he wrote on a rainy day, for example,
the rain got incorporated into his story. Most writers are aware
that they incorporate outside occurrences from time to time. In
principle, it's not much different from spinning a wheel to decide
what happens next.

It would be simple to put a writer's plot wheel on a computer.
But that wouldn't help much, because the instructions on the
wheel are just spurs to creativity. A phrase such as "Get knocked
out" merely jogs the creative energies of the writer. In fact, incorporating an external event and making it one's own is the creative
part of the process—not the external event itself. The more I
thought about it, the more the spinning wheel seemed like a joke.*

Isn't it possible to imagine a machine that could do something
more? Can't a machine be given enough rules and information to
enable it to tell us stories? Yes, it can. That's been done several
times. The trouble is that the stories aren't interesting.

What makes an interesting story? In an interesting story, we
want to know what happens next—because we have identified, in

*I finally wrote a little program as a joke. It's in the appendices.

some way, with the characters in the story. We are able to identify with characters of a different sex, or from a different time. We can identify with unpleasant characters, even characters that we hate. The process of identification is complex, but there is something ineluctably human about it. Machines can't create the conditions for that identification in us—because they are machines.

In saying this, I am not making a philosophical point, but a practical one. It is indisputable that machines can imitate many aspects of human behavior, and can proceed in ways indistinguishable from human procedures in limited situations. But the formal rules for playing chess are simple compared with the formal rules for writing tragedy—assuming such formal rules exist at all. I suspect they do, but that doesn't mean that they can be discovered in any easy way. Even when human stories follow obvious genre formulas, we distinguish between a good use of the formula and a bad one. What makes the difference? Nobody really knows. Even the most perceptive critics are talking about behavior that they themselves cannot duplicate. What hope is there for the computer programmer? I think, as a practical matter, none.

If true computer music were ever written, it would only be listened to by other computers. I think this is an inherent limitation that we prefer to ignore.

For example, there has been a great popular interest in extraterrestrial life in the past decade. It has caught the imagination of the entire society, from scientists to moviemakers. But the fact is that all conceptions of alien life are basically like us. Those rubbery cute little guys are just that—rubbery cute little human beings. There are stranger life forms already on our own planet. And the biases that configured the plaque on Pioneer 10 are little better concealed, although there was at least an attempt to be more general. What's interesting is that the attempt failed; it always fails.

You can't get the human bias out of the human imagination. All we can imagine are variations of ourselves, because nothing else makes sense to us. We see what we know, and we imagine what we can imagine. Human art is inevitably human.

Radically different art would be literally invisible. I've often been amused to think that domestic dogs practice an art form, right under our noses. After all, a dog walking down a street behaves just like a person in an art gallery, going from picture to picture, alert and interested. There's a whole world of fascination for dogs that we can't participate in, because we have no comparable sense of smell.

Less fancifully, Edmund Carpenter* tells how seventeenth-century sailors enjoyed inviting aborigines aboard their ships and firing off cannons unexpectedly to scare them. But when the cannons were fired, the Indians didn't even blink. They had no reaction at all. The loud sound meant nothing to them.

What is truly new does not create shock—it creates nothing. If we are shocked by art, we are shocked because our expectations are not met. And that means we already have expectations based on previous experience.

Is there anything, then, that can be called computer art? I think there is. I think that certain products of the search for artificial intelligence—programs such as ELIZA and SHRDLU—are computer art.

By computer art I don't mean the computer made them; I mean they are human artworks possible only with a computer. Why are they human artworks?

First of all, they are handmade creations, often beautifully done. They aren't the inevitable consequence of a scientific theory; they are ad hoc constructions by human beings.

Second, they create a little world, akin to medieval miniature paintings. Within this little world, everything conforms to the artist's (programmer's) perception of how that world works, and they are internally consistent—one of the hallmarks of a work of art.

Third, they reflect back to us something about the outer

*Carpenter, Edmund. *Oh, What a Blow That Phantom Gave Me!* (New York: Bantam, 1974), p. 33.

or "real" world that this inner world partially describes in a simplified form. In this respect, too, they are clearly works of art, since all art is a simplified version of some larger reality.

Finally, they inevitably show the traces of their creator. Even if a team of people has built the program, the team has operated under someone's instruction and guidance. That person has a world view that is reflected in the final program.

If one imagines artificial-intelligence programs as an art form, then many objections to them disappear (and perhaps much funding). We don't complain that the Sistine Chapel ceiling is not also *The Last Supper.* The very idea is absurd. Art is inherently limited; we appreciate it for what it is, not what it isn't.

For example, SHRDLU was a doctoral thesis by Terry Winograd, a brilliant artificial-intelligence worker. SHRDLU operates in a limited world in which a robot arm moves blocks and other forms on a tabletop. (There are no actual blocks or robot arm; the world is all imaginary, though it is represented graphically.) The following interaction of SHRDLU is reported by Joseph Weizenbaum.

> HUMAN: Find a block which is taller than the one you are holding and put it in the box.
>
> ROBOT: By "it" I assume you mean the block which is taller than the one I am holding.
>
> HUMAN: O.K.
>
> ROBOT: (The hand sets down the block it is holding and picks up a taller one.)
>
> HUMAN: What does the box contain?
>
> ROBOT: The blue pyramid and the blue box.
>
> HUMAN: What is the pyramid supported by?
>
> ROBOT: The box.
>
> HUMAN: Why did you clear off (the red) cube?
>
> ROBOT: To put it on a large green cube.
>
> HUMAN: Why did you do that?
>
> ROBOT: To stack up the red cube, a large red block, and a large green cube.

HUMAN: Why did you do that?
ROBOT: Because you asked me to.

SHRDLU is so remarkable that it seems uncharitable to point out that the program can't tell you who won the football game, whether it's raining outside, or who's the President of the United States. SHRDLU only functions in its little world of boxes on the tabletop. It can't step outside this miniature world at all. It's like an elaborate nineteenth-century clockwork mechanism where little figures dance on a little landscape. It's wonderful for what it is—and it represents only a small part of the vastness of the real world.

Problems arise from the claims made for SHRDLU and other programs, since the avowed purpose of artificial-intelligence studies is to produce just that, a genuine artificial intelligence. But there's no reason to dismiss these beautiful creations because their makers overstate their significance. Leonardo da Vinci insisted he was a scientist representing reality according to natural laws. In a sense he was, but not in the same sense as Galileo, who made an identical claim for his activities.

We have learned the wisdom of appreciating works of art for what they mean to us, not paying too much attention to what the creators think they mean. In recent years we've come to treat science and technology in the same way. This is healthy and sane.

Computer-Assisted

This phrase is heaven-sent for acronym collectors. It offers such variants as CAD, Computer-Assisted Design;* CAI, Computer-Assisted Instruction; CAM, Computer-Assisted Manufacturing;

*Some insist CAD stands for Computer-Assisted Delay.

CADE, Computer-Assisted Data Entry; CAT, Computer-Assisted Teaching, Testing, or Tomography; CASE, Computer-Assisted Software Engineering or Computer-Assisted Systems Evaluation. . . . Had enough?

But there are so many more we haven't covered.

Actually, I've got one of my own—CACA, for Computer-Assisted Crap Analysis. If you feed caca into CACA, you come out with caca. This verifies the oldest computer axiom, "Garbage in, garbage out."

Acronyms are the SPOOR (Self-Perpetuating Organizational Operating Regimentation) of the bureaucratic brain. A snappy acronym becomes a thing-in-itself and obscures direct meaning. This is often beneficial to the creators of the thing-in-itself—and they know it. These people aren't fools.

So be cautious with Computer-Assisted Anything. Remember that in Computer-Assisted Design or Teaching, it's the Design and the Teaching that matter, and the Computer Assistant at best only Assists. It may not even do that.

Keep the converse in mind. If your Computer-Assisted Teaching system operates well, it's because a person worked damn hard to make the programs good, not because the machines supplied some magic on their own.

Never forget: computers are machines developed by people, programmed by people, fed information by people, and operated by people. What comes out of this Computer-Assisted-Chain-Letter Exercise (CACLE) reflects human characteristics far more than machine characteristics.

The day may come when we will consult artificial intelligences that will make a real contribution toward solving our problems. But don't look for it now. You'd be better off whispering sweet nothings into the tail pipe of a Chevrolet.

Computer Crime

In seventeenth-century England, more than two hundred crimes were punishable by hanging. The great majority of those felonies were crimes against property; stealing goods worth more than a shilling was sufficient for the death sentence.

The only way to avoid hanging was by royal pardon or "benefit of clergy"—a convicted criminal had the right to call for a Bible, and if he could read it aloud to the court, he was branded on the thumb and released. Benefit of clergy was originally a medieval notion, dating from the time when priests were the only literate members of society, and were subject to their own ecclesiastical courts.

But remnants of this medieval tradition persist to this day in modern attitudes toward white-collar crime. We are reluctant to define white-collar crime as crime at all; the milk-toast bank clerk who embezzles, or the corporate high roller with a Bahamas bank account, is likely to get off with a slap on the wrist, if he is prosecuted at all.

Such criminals appear to us quite different from the brutal street mugger who presses a gun to his victim's head. White-collar "criminals" are nicely dressed, responsible, and educated. They steal from large, faceless institutions, such as banks and insurance companies, which can afford the losses. Privately, we resent the large institutions of society; anybody who rips off the IRS or the telephone company is likely to be viewed as a clever, praiseworthy person.

It is into this protective misperception of white-collar crime that the computer criminal neatly fits. The computer criminal enjoys further advantages. Few like computers and fewer still understand them; the computer criminal is perceived as unusually bright and smart. Furthermore, the computer criminal is often young and without serious criminal intent. When a teenager taps into Defense Department data banks, we perceive humiliation of the government, and we're delighted. The fact that it costs the DOD $24 million to untangle the mess is hardly worth mentioning. And if another teenager taps into the high-school records to change his girlfriend's grades, that's just a youthful prank. We remember how it was.

Of course this is all nonsense.

Institutions pass their losses on; ultimately we pay for the depredations of computer criminals—an amount estimated at from $5 billion to $30 billion a year.

If we stopped to think about it, we would not be amused by Alec Guinness as the embezzling bank clerk, Liza Minnelli as the shoplifter, or Peter Ustinov as the computer criminal.

In fact, the long-standing leniency toward white-collar crime is about to undergo a startling revision. A company like Citibank uses computers to process transactions amounting to $30 billion a day for customers in a hundred different countries. American banks move $400 billion a day by computer just within the United States. Our society is now simply too vulnerable to disruption to view white-collar crime tolerantly. Among the changes:

Institutions will lose their embarrassment about their self-image—the chief reason computer prosecutions are rare. Computer crime is not evidence of mismanagement; it's evidence of crime.

Companies will abandon their naïveté about employee honesty. Many companies seem to think that their employees won't steal because they're good Americans and loyal to the company. Yet a substantial body of psychological data suggests that people will do whatever they can get away with. The best guarantee of employees' honesty is a system that doesn't tempt them.

We will be less inclined to regard computer crime as clever. Most computer crime is rather stupidly simpleminded. The welfare worker who programs the computer to make out checks to himself isn't smart. (If he were smart, he wouldn't send the checks to his own house.) Nor is computer crime innocent. The disgruntled employee who programs a logic bomb in the computer to shut down the system a month after he leaves is no better than an arsonist.

Further, as more people become skilled in the use of computers, the vulnerability of individuals will increase. It's one thing to read that someone ripped off the phone company. It's another thing to have an argument with your neighbor, who then taps into data banks and destroys your credit rating, eliminates bank records of your mortgage payments, or orders your car repossessed.

Finally, age will cease to be a mitigating factor. The ability of some kid to shut down a large computer system in another city or another country for a week or two will simply be intolerable —no matter how much he explains that he didn't mean it. After a period of education in these matters, there will be several highly publicized cases in which twelve-year-olds go to jail. Everybody's going to feel uncomfortable about it, but society won't really have a choice.

Along with a change in attitudes will be a change in the way data is handled. With the breaking of the Stanford public key code in 1982, it has finally become clear that encryption alone can't provide adequate security. Other sophisticated techniques will be added. Internal watchdog programs will track communications inside a system, looking for suspicious interactions. Biometric verifications will be increasingly common—checking fingerprints, retinal blood-vessel patterns, handwriting, or voice—before a user is allowed access to a system.

Large institutions are already hardening their security in traditional ways. Major data banks won't be accessible on open telephone lines much longer; there will be separate systems for transmitting information—the electronic extension of the bank vault. Institutions that fail to take these measures will get what they deserve. Before 1982, the biggest single computer theft was $10.2 million, but in that year Wells Fargo was hit for $21.3 million.

If you don't want anybody to get his hands on your money or your information, you'd better make sure it's not available. The tendency to lock up important information will pervade the society to a degree previously unknown.

Configuration

Computerese for exactly what you have. There are so many possible modifications to a computer, so many different input and output devices, and so many ways to describe the resulting configuration, that there is only one solution: make a list and carry it with you.

The list should include the name and model of your machine, and any modifications; the name, model, and slot number of any additional hardware boards or interface boards; the name and model of peripherals, and any enhancements; and so on.*

Keep this list handy when you visit a store or call for help. Even if it means nothing to you, it'll make sense to whomever you're talking to. There's nothing more frustrating—for you and the other person—than not knowing what equipment you have, and how it is configured.

Control over the Computer

Fred Astaire once said that whenever he bought new clothes, he took them home and threw them against the wall a couple of times

---

*As an example, here is the list for an Apple:

ITEM	MANUFACTURER	SLOT
Apple II Plus	Apple Computer	—
CP/M Card	Microsoft RAMCARD	#0
Serial Printer Card	Model 7710-A (AS-1)	#1
80 Column Card	Videx	#3

—just to get the intimidating *newness* out of them, and to show them who was boss.

Some people fret over a new car until it gets its first ding in the door. Then they relax: it becomes just another car. (I have a clever friend who parks his new car in tight spaces so that he'll get a ding right away.) Many people, on taking up a new residence, immediately cook their favorite dish to get familiar smells into the place.

These are all ways of asserting control over a new object or situation.

People have a similar desire to assert control over a computer, but they're unsure how to proceed. Throwing it against the wall or dinging the case is unwise. And merely running store-bought programs is insufficient; even after a year, you'll feel some lingering unease.

In my experience, you assert control over a computer—show it who's boss—by making it do something unique. That means programming it. Even if you never want to program again in your life, if you devote a couple of hours to programming a new machine, you'll feel better about it ever afterward.

So set aside some quiet time, open your machine's instruction manual, and follow along. Don't feel discouraged if you are doing simple things. Complexity is not the point. The point is familiarity.

(I've included a simple, take-control routine for the Apple computer and the IBM Personal Computer in the appendices of this book.)

ITEM	MANUFACTURER	SLOT
Language Card	Microsoft	#4
Disk Controller Card	Apple Computer	#6
2 Disk Drives	Apple Computer	—
Monitor	Amdek 300	—
Printer	IDS 460	—

Convert, Computer

As with the reformed hooker or ex-smoker, beware the zeal of the computer convert. The most vigorous opponent of the machine usually becomes its most intemperate advocate.

In reality, you're seeing two extremes of the same neurosis. The person who deeply resists computers is insecure. His sense of control over his life and work is shaky; he is a person drowning in a lack of self-worth. And, contrary to popular opinion, chronically drowning people don't grasp at any straw; they're far more likely to deny they're drowning at all.

However, given a solid straw, the drowning person embraces it in a death grip. Nothing will shake him loose from this newly perceived salvation. Having insisted the computer is totally useless, he now feels the computer solves all of life's problems.

He wasn't right before, and he's still not right. A computer, like any other human creation, has advantages and disadvantages. View it in a balanced way.

Copyright

Copyright is literally that—the right to copy. For valuable information, possession of copyright is the traditional method to obtain payment for the work that went into creation.

The history of copyright law reflects the history of copying techniques. The printing press spurred the first copyrights for the authors of written works. Later, copyright law was extended to cover musical compositions and photographic works as problems with copying those creations arose.

But as recently as three years ago, computer programs were not protected by copyright law. Although that position is no longer tenable, the exact application of copyright law to computer programs is unclear. Meanwhile, new technological developments have made copyright law increasingly awkward in other areas.

For more than twenty years, authors and publishers have fought the ability of individuals to Xerox written works at will. But it's clear that methods for copying text are slow, difficult, and expensive. Anyone who wants to Xerox a book must spend a lot of time at it. The copy cost will probably exceed the cost of buying the book itself. Additional copies are nearly as expensive and as time-consuming as the first one. Thus the threat of Xerox technology has always been limited by practical considerations.

Similarly, anyone who wants to make a 35-mm photographic copy of a movie has his work cut out for him. The film stock costs one thousand dollars and the technique requires a roomful of specialized equipment. It can be done, but not conveniently.

But once information is transferred to an electronic form, copying the information becomes extremely easy. One can tape a record album or a televised movie with no effort. Multiple copies can be run off from the original. And while it is true that the cost of raw materials is a substantial fraction of the original—audiotape costs half the price of an album, and videotape costs a quarter the price of a taped movie—the savings are sufficient to make the effort worthwhile. Losses from copying records and movies may amount to hundreds of millions of dollars a year; no one knows for sure how much.

The public tends to shrug off such theft. After all, Mozart and John Ford are dead and won't care if we tape their creations; and people are not inclined to sympathize if Rod Stewart or Clint Eastwood loses a few pennies from individual acts of piracy, since these artists are perceived as incredibly overpaid in the first place.

But when we come to computer programs, the ramifications of unrestricted copying become very great indeed. A computer program is a complex creation, often involving many people over a period of years. The programs may sell for a thousand dollars or more. Yet one can copy such an expensive program onto a two-dollar floppy disk in thirty seconds or less. The difference in cost between purchasing and stealing is enormous. And if one puts the pirated program out on a computer network, thousands of other people can instantly make copies, too. Losses in the annual $200 million American software market are estimated at from $12 million to $36 million.

Predictably, groups affected by this new copying technology have sought to preserve copyright protection in some semblance of its traditional form. Authors and motion picture producers have asked the courts to outlaw copying technology, or to tax it at the point of sale. Computer program manufacturers have devised elaborate techniques to prevent copying of disks, although these efforts have merely created a parallel industry devoted to breaking each new copy-protection technique. Any computer-wise kid will tell you flatly, "You can copy *anything.*"

Whatever the courts decide in the short term, it will eventually be obvious that there is no way to regulate widespread copying in an electronic information society. The technology can't be stopped; consumer preference for videotape over laser disks means, bluntly, that people *want* to copy.* They are beginning to think of it as an ordinary right. A tax on copying technology at some early point will never be equitable. The problem will only get worse.

Buckminster Fuller argued that we should use forces, not fight them. The problem of copyright looks somewhat different the moment one accepts copying technology as uncontrollable.

Copyright actually has two aspects. The first is payment for dissemination; the second is protection against the dissemination of competing, essentially identical products. Only this second aspect will remain a recognizable legal issue. Payment for dissemination *must* take a new form. Given the fact that extensive networks already exist to spread electronic information—radio stations,

---

*It may also mean that they want to show pornographic movies at home. But that isn't clear. Sooner or later, somebody would make pornographic laser disks. But one thing was clear: you'd never be able to copy with laser disks. For most consumers, that was the end of the discussion.

cable TV systems, and computer networks—we must conceive new ideas of dissemination. Old ideas presumed a life span for the information. For example, a movie could be shown in domestic theaters, then foreign theaters, then on airplanes, then on pay TV, and finally on network TV. All this might take five years.

But dissemination has now become instantaneous. Once the information is released in any form, copying inevitably follows. There were illegal videotapes of *E.T.* for sale the day the film opened in the American movie theaters; they circulated in England for six months before the film opened, and theater revenues correspondingly fell.

The only solution is to accept instantaneous dissemination as a fact of electronic life. The creators of a movie, a musical composition, or a computer program will come to recognize only two stages of its existence—absolute private ownership during development, and absolute public ownership at the moment of release. The dividing line will be sharply defined, and the creator will receive all of his compensation when he crosses it.*

Some consequences of this new scheme should be stated explicitly. First, there must be competing networks of dissemination to prevent monopolies. This is already recognized as a potential problem, and is the reason film companies are creating cable TV companies to compete with the monolithic Home Box Office.

Second, people will still go to movies and concerts and plays, but it'll be understood that they are paying for a method of reproduction, and not access to the information itself.

Third, absolute public ownership will not be identical to what we now call public domain. The authors of a computer program or a movie will reserve certain rights to their creation, particularly the right to make updates or sequels. Exactly what these rights

---

*This does not mean an end to royalties. Creators will still be paid as a function of the audience they attract. Cable TV or computer networks can keep track of their viewers or users and pay creators accordingly. But although you must pay for the first night's viewing of a movie on cable, there's nothing to prevent you from copying it and viewing it again, or lending the copy to a neighbor. Just as there is now nothing to prevent you from lending a book or a magazine to your neighbor.

consist of will be bitterly fought in the courts during the next ten years; the battles have already begun.

It is by no means clear how these legal issues will be resolved. But it seems inevitable that our ideas of ownership and copying of information will undergo radical revision in the coming years. Because they have to.

Courseware

This hideous neologism is a mark of the computer Calvinist, as the cloven hoof is the mark of the Devil. Refuse all courseware offered to you.

Don't be fooled by institutions with intellectual traditions; traditions don't apply to computers, and as a matter of fact traditional college professorware seems to be in the vanguard of forcing courseware upon unsuspecting students.

Remember that education imparts not only facts, but an organizational framework for those facts—a way of looking at the body of knowledge. This framework is much more powerful than the facts themselves, which is why students remember their professors vividly long after they've forgotten the specific content of the classes.

But the framework is usually unconscious and inexplicit. There are often hidden agendas at work. Employing unnecessary or phony jargon—such as "courseware"—may imply that the teacher wishes to make the information more specialized and difficult than it really is. An instructor who needs to emphasize his own superiority over the hapless student is not a good teacher. Students need someone who will demystify the information, and make it easy to learn as possible.

Take a regular, old-fashioned class from a regular, old-fashioned teacher—and skip the academic posturing.

Creative

"The computer isn't creative—what good is it to me?" say a lot of my friends who are artists and composers and writers. This is a remarkably stupid attitude.

No, a computer is not creative. Nor is a typewriter, a piano, or a paintbrush. They are tools, and everybody uses them. (Well, not everybody. You still hear some writers insist that real stylists don't compose on a typewriter, as if pushing a pencil had some magical effect on prose. This is basically a nineteenth-century snobbism, and it overlooks inconvenient truths such as the fact that the first novel written on a typewriter was *The Adventures of Tom Sawyer.* Mark Twain, no fool, didn't make that widely known. See STATUS, COMPUTERS AND.)

Creative people tend to focus on the uniquely difficult parts of their work—the parts that drive them crazy, the parts they are anxious about—and they conclude, correctly, that computers can't help with those parts. Nobody and no thing can help.

But more mundane aspects of their work *would* benefit from help. For example, a film-composer friend, after investigating different computerized music systems, said to me, "I can't see how they would help me, given the way I work. I just have to sit at the piano and scratch it out."

Yet it was clear that he repeatedly faced irritating minor problems. Sometimes the arranger couldn't read his handwritten score; a legible printout would help. Film scores have to be precisely written to the second; sometimes he lost or added a beat, and later had to make adjustments in a rush. In fact, he lived with a constant nagging anxiety that he'd mistimed a piece of music. Then, too, the film was frequently recut at the last minute, forcing him to add or delete a few bars under great pressure. At such times he was especially likely to make mistakes.

The point is that these aspects of his work were not perceived as "part of the job." His job was to compose; the exasperating details were just the price he paid to do the work he loved.

Yet these problems *were* part of the job—at least, they sapped his energy and time—and they were a snap for a computer. He got one. And, as inevitably happens, as soon as he had the machine he began to discover one or two other things that had always annoyed him and that he wanted to fix. . . .

My own view is that creative people need computers more than others, if only to handle the tedious, routine aspects of their work, to give them more time to create. (Creative people often glorify these mundane details, because they think they have to do them.)

Render unto the machine what is the machine's. You go do what only a human being can do.

Debugging

Programs never work the first time.

In the earliest days of computers, this fact came as a big surprise. People imagined that they would simply write a program, put it on the computer, and it would run. It took a while to realize that a debugging period invariably followed the introduction of any new program.

The whole idea of debugging puts people off, though I don't know why. Writers often say that books aren't written, they're rewritten. And in fact most formal assemblies of information—proposals, applications, speeches, presentations, designs—go through several drafts or revisions. So there's nothing unique about rewriting for a computer. Think of the debugging process as a creative period in which you refine your ideas. And realize that debugging is never finished. (See TESTING.)

Dedicated Machines

Originally, a dedicated machine was one that required a dedicated electrical line—meaning a separate power line drawing directly from the source, and therefore dedicated to one particular outlet. The first dedicated machines were word processors and other specialized computers intended to handle specific tasks; the early models of these machines could not tolerate minor electrical fluctuations on a non-dedicated electrical line.

Dedicated machines are sneered at by computer Calvinists, who think that a single-purpose machine is somehow cheating. But the advantages of such a machine should not be underestimated.

The true computer lacks a specific purpose; the same machine can balance your checkbook, check spelling on your letters, and play Space Invaders with the kids. But this versatility is not without its drawbacks; even among computers, the jack-of-all-trades is master of none.

Specialized machines sacrifice versatility in favor of additional features applicable to a specific use. Everything about these machines, from keyboard to disk drives to monitor, is designed with that one use in mind. They are also often cheaper than a comparable general computer.* Some major categories to consider are:

WORD PROCESSING

If you're a professional writer, or if you have a business where all you really want is word processing, buy a dedicated word processor. It will do a far better job than the best word-processing program for a general computer, and it will be much easier to learn to use.

*The IBM Displaywriter, a dedicated word processor, is two hundred dollars cheaper than a comparably equipped IBM Personal Computer.

MUSIC COMPOSITION

Machines combining electronic synthesizers and computer memory are a natural. If you're interested in music and can afford a specialized machine, buy one.

LABORATORY APPLICATIONS

If you want to monitor instruments and process analog input, get a machine built to do that job. Much laboratory disaffection with personal computers arises from the hassle of adapting a general-purpose machine to specialized needs. It's hard enough to get an experimental prep running smoothly; who needs the additional bother of making a personal computer interface with it?

INFORMATION NETWORKS

If you want Dow Jones or The Source or any other information network, get an interface device and be done with it.

GAMES

You can save a lot of time and some money by buying a game console that plugs into your television. Any child can tell you the pros and cons of different systems.

CALCULATION

If all you want is a sophisticated calculator, you can buy for about a hundred dollars a handheld machine that can be programmed in BASIC and that has a typewriter keyboard, a built-in printer, and a small memory for words and numbers.

In thinking about dedicated machines, bear in mind the question of availability to the user. My sister bought an Apple II for herself and her teenage daughter, but because my sister uses it constantly for word processing, her daughter has no chance to get on it. They need two machines.

Many labs buy a personal computer because it can do word processing, but the machine is constantly monitoring laboratory experiments that cannot be interrupted, so its value for word processing is nil. These labs would be better off with a word processor and a separate laboratory monitor.

A machine is no good to you if you can't get on it. If you have two distinct full-time needs, you need two machines.

I suspect we'll see more dedicated machines in the future. Trends in chip construction suggest it will become easier to make specialized machines. Especially important is the ability of the special-purpose manufacturer to design his own VLSI (Very Large Scale Integration) computer chip.

A VLSI computer chip is defined as a chip so complex that it cannot be designed by a single engineer in his lifetime. VLSI design has become heavily automated, using what are now called "silicon compilers" to aid in creating the design. As a result, specialized VLSI chips can be designed for specialized machines, even if only a few thousand chips are turned out—or even a few hundred. The trend toward specialized manufacture at the level of the silicon chip is bound to increase the range and availability of special machines.

Indeed, it may turn out that the general-purpose computer is a creation unique to the late twentieth century. It may soon be practical to have one computer for doing graphics, another for doing word processing, another to link with our interactive cable TV, and so on.*

In any case, don't let the computer Calvinists make you feel you're a sissy because you've bought a special machine that does the job. The whole idea of machines is to do the job.

---

*There is a counter-argument, based on the history of digital watches and calculators. Those devices have shown a clear trend toward incorporating more and more functions into a single device. People now take it for granted that they can buy a calculator that will tell them the day, date, and time in multiple time zones; that functions as a stopwatch with a lap timer; that has an alarm; that plays musical tunes; that stores a little text; and that even provides a game or two.

But even though their calculators tell time, most people still wear wristwatches.

Design

The earliest designs of any new object reflect older images. The first Pulsar digital watches looked like TV sets; the first home computers looked like typewriters mating with TV sets.

External computer design is still dominated by engineers, and there are a lot of ugly clunkers around. But there's no excuse for making a machine that looks like a toilet on the space shuttle—and less excuse for buying one. I'm constantly surprised that people who wouldn't put an ugly stereo on a side shelf will place one of these junky boxes right in the center of their desk, as if they had no choice.

Apple, Atari, IBM, DEC, Epson, Xerox, and Olivetti make pleasant-looking computers, although they're all basically white or gray. (I don't know why computers don't come in colors; eventually they will.)

Good design is not an aesthetic frill; it matters. A pleasing appearance means somebody cared how it looks to you; it's a strong hint that the inner workings have been arranged with the user in mind, too.

Digital

Everything's digital these days, but it wasn't always so.

In 1973, I made a movie called *Westworld,* which was a fantasy about robots. The film required us to show the point of view of the main robot, played by Yul Brynner. But what special-effects technique would best suggest a machine's point of view?

I proposed a rather simple solution: to show the point of view of a machine, use a machine. I wanted to film the scenes and then manipulate the film with a computer.

This process of converting a photographic image for machine

use is called *digitizing.* In essence, an electric eye attached to the machine scans the image in small units, called *pixels,* and assigns each pixel a numerical value. The picture is thus converted into a series of numbers, and the numbers can be manipulated in different ways.

Once the manipulation is completed, the process is reversed—the machine takes the digital information and reconstitutes a picture.

Such a process had never been used for motion picture films before, and none of the special-effects houses even knew what we were talking about. At this time, film special effects were limited to purely photographic processes such as solarization—the technique used, for example, to make the shimmery, bizarre-colored landscapes in *2001.* None of the special-effects houses had computers or were even thinking about them; all they could do were variations on photographic techniques. But photographic techniques look like just that—darkroom manipulation of the filmed image. I wanted a mechanical process.

Finally we went to the Jet Propulsion Laboratory in Pasadena. At least they knew what we were talking about. They explained that the technique had thus far only been used for single images, because each required massive computer power. We were talking about two minutes of film, or 2,880 separate images. But they said they could do it: they could process two minutes of movie film. It would take nine months and cost $200,000.

Since the entire film had to be finished and released in six months, at a total cost of $1 million, we had to look elsewhere. Eventually John Whitney, Jr., agreed to undertake the job in four months for $20,000. He used the machines at Information International, Inc., a local business with lots of computer power. Triple-I had vast rooms full of mainframe machines. But it was still brutally difficult. We had to shoot the film under special conditions to assist the computer in reading it. Then each frame of film had to be broken down into its three color separations, and each separation frame had to be scanned individually, a process that took hours. Working long hours and nights with the giant mainframes, John was able to process only a few seconds of film a week.

But in the end, we got what we needed. *Westworld* was the first feature film to process imagery by computer. We obtained a sort of blocky, animated effect that was remarkable in 1973—and a cliché seven years later, when similar imagery appeared in everything from perfume ads to paintings by Salvador Dali.

But the point is that proliferation of this computer-processed imagery has been matched by a substantial proliferation of computer power. Computer animation for commercials and logos is now a thriving business, and small shops crank them out with tiny, very powerful micros. These days the most expensive film in the world is the three-second logos for network television. Those rotating, glinting ABC and NBC letters are entirely created by computer, and cost about $25,000 a second.

Even feature films such as *Star Wars* that rely on photographic special effects use small computers in dozens of different ways: running the cameras, controlling exposures, operating the optical printers, and so on. Although we don't think about it, such films would be impossible without substantial computer power. They are entertainment products of the computer age.

Disk, Floppy

Floppy disks are the most common storage medium for small computers. Think of them as audio cassettes pressed flat, like records. They're roughly as durable as audio cassettes.

Experts warn you to treat floppies with care: they shouldn't be bent, exposed to extreme temperature, dust, liquids, or electromagnetic radiation. Mail or airport security checks may injure them. As a result, anxious beginners handle floppies as if they were made of glass.

Yet in practice, floppies tolerate substantial abuse. Even if you smear your greasy fingers on the center hole,* jam them into the

---

*I've never understood why women, far more than men, seem to handle floppy disks by putting their index fingers through the center hole. In any case, man or woman, it's a bad idea. Handle a disk on the rectangular outer folder only.

disk drive, and dribble cigarette ash on them, they'll probably still work. You can mail them and take them on airplanes with no problem. They're not really so fragile.

However, like audio cassettes, *they fail without warning.* One minute you're playing your favorite audiotape in your car; the next minute, you're untangling a snarl of brown ribbon. Floppy disks show the same unpredictability. Therefore you should always have a backup copy of any important disk.

Beginning users invariably ignore this advice—until they have their first disaster. Indeed, one minor puzzle of computers is that people don't back up their data until they personally experience a nasty screwup.

A friend of mine had six months of small-business accounts on one disk. The disk was lying next to the keyboard when he knocked his gin and tonic over on it one evening, soaking the disk. He had no backup copy. Result: night after night retyping the data into the computer.

I had a hundred pages of a screenplay on a disk when something happened—a power surge, a write error in the drive, a flaw on the disk surface itself, *something*—and the disk became suddenly unusable. I couldn't recover it, I couldn't print out its contents, I couldn't copy it, I couldn't do anything. I sent it to the intensive-care unit of the manufacturer; they returned it with regrets. It was a dead disk. I had no copy.

A friend returned home to find his teething eight-month-old daughter chewing on one of his disks. He had no copy.

Another friend's offspring carefully put Daddy's disks to one side while they played. Unfortunately, the disks were placed beside a toy ray gun containing a powerful magnet. Result: erased disks. He had copies, all right, but the copies were erased along with the originals.

Every computer user has his own disaster story. The lesson is simple. Make a backup copy of anything you care about. Keep your copies separate from the originals. It's not a bad idea to make two backups of important disks.

Disks are cheaper than time. Learn to think of every disk as actually two disks—the original and its backup copy.

Back up your data.

. . .

Two facts about floppy disks that aren't widely known:

New disks contain defects about as often as audio records or tapes. If you've just bought a program that doesn't run according to the instructions, your first suspicion should be that the disk is defective. Don't assume you're doing something wrong. Don't waste a weekend trying to make it work. Take it back to the store and exchange it.

Also, your own data disks may prove defective—and that may not become evident until the disk has been used for some time. If a disk begins to act up consistently, copy its contents onto a new disk, and throw the defective disk out. Don't copy it onto your existing backup. (See RECOVERY.)

Some terminology:

Disks come in *single- or double-density* varieties. This simply refers to how densely the data can be laid down on them.

Disks have an internal architecture that involves *sectors* and *tracks.* Forget about all that unless you plan serious programming. Your machine will *format* a new disk to its specific requirements automatically; you don't need to involve yourself in the details. Leave that to your machine and your disk.

The term *diskette* is meaningless. The first mylar disks for computer storage were 14 inches in diameter, so when the 8-inch version was introduced, they were called diskettes. Then 5¼-inch disks were introduced, and *they* were called diskettes. Now Sony has come out with a new 3½-inch diskette. It seems time simply to call everything a disk. Why use a longer word when a short one will do?

Finally, a most troublesome piece of computer jargon is the word *boot.* The term has a historical rationale, but nowadays to boot a disk or a system usually means to insert the disk and turn the computer on.

Disk, Laser

Laser disks were originally invented for recording photographic information, but they have enormous data-storage capacity as well. One laser disk the size of an LP record can store a billion words, which is more than the average person will read in his entire life.

Programs have been written to enable computers to control laser-disk recorders. Such combinations of computer and laser disk offer considerable potential. As I write this, arcade games are starting to use laser disks to provide photographic-quality images for the gamester as he swoops, bombs, and torpedoes his way through life.

But more serious applications of the laser disk lie further in the future. At the moment, there are problems with disk manufacture, and playback equipment is expensive. And the programming challenges presented by such enormous storage capacity are, to say the least, daunting.

Documentation

Computerese for instructions. The quality of the instructions for a program is nearly as important as the program itself, since it determines how quickly and effectively you will learn to use the program. Many otherwise excellent programs have astoundingly bad instructions.

Look for several things.

First, does the documentation provide a general explanation, telling you about the program and what it does? Such general orientation is always valuable.

Second, does it provide step-by-step examples of how to use the program? Does it have pictures showing how the screen looks as you go step by step? It is easiest to learn a new program by following a provided example.

Third, does it have an index? Documentation without an index will eventually drive you wild. The beginning user is most often focused on learning how to use the program, and may ignore the fact that once learned, the documentation is then only an occasional reference—and a reference without an index is frustrating.

Finally, if it is a complex program, does it have a compact reference card to keep by the machine while you work?

The best documentation seems to have some sections that are absurdly clear and some sections that are forbiddingly complex. If you can't understand any of it, then the documentation is probably too technical. If you understand all of it right away, then it'll probably prove too superficial for long-term use.

Many people are embarrassed to admit they want idiot-simple instructions. This embarrassment is more acute if you already have some familiarity with machines and programs. But the fact that you're a whiz with word processing means nothing when you look at an accounting package or a data-base management program. There's no disgrace in wanting instructions that begin, "Put in the disk and turn on your machine. See the little blinking light. That is the cursor. . . ." Quite the contrary, it makes excellent sense. The simpler it is, the faster you'll learn, and the faster you learn, the sooner you'll be able to use the program—which is the point.

Finally, ask if the program has additional instructions written by someone else. Many popular but poorly documented programs —such as Wordstar—now have exemplary instructions sold in book form by outside people. These are nearly always worth the money.

Just as disks are often defective, documentation is often wrong. Having another source of documentation can save hours of frustration trying to make the program do something that is badly or incorrectly explained in the original documentation. After you've blown Sunday at the keyboard, you won't be glad to go to the computer shop on Monday and be told, "Oh yeah, the documentation is wrong on that point. You have to press Control-F-U and it works fine."

. . .

Documentation has the additional meaning of explanations inserted within the body of a program to tell you what a given line of computer code means.

Such documentation is essential if others are to pick up where the original programmer left off. It's difficult to decipher the thinking of a programmer months or years after the original work was done.

This applies to you, too.

If you decide to program, just wait until you work on something into the wee hours—and then try to decipher what you've done the very next morning. You won't believe it. It's like a magic trick: you haven't any idea what was in your mind just a few hours before.

This problem is not confined to novices. Terry Winograd, the brilliant author of the artificial-intelligence program SHRDLU, was unable to modify his program a few years later, because neither he nor anyone else could figure it out.*

An undocumented program is unmodifiable and therefore of limited value. Standards for program documentation have become more demanding in recent years. It is now common practice to insert an explanatory comment for each line of computer instruction.

Dog, Feeding the

Will your computer feed the dog? Will it take out the trash? Baby-sit the kids? If it won't, then what good is it?

The answer is that any personal computer *can* do all these things. A few enterprising souls employ computers to manage their households to an extraordinary degree, but they've had to

---

*SHRDLU was of course documented, but it was a long program (more than 250,000 lines of code) and the documentation was inadequate to allow revisions.

work at it. At the moment there is no commercially available Dog-Feeding Peripheral (DFP). But the DFP is surely in the cards. I've been tempted to build the prototype myself, just to silence cynical friends.

A lowly Apple computer with 48K of memory can run all the operations of an offshore-drilling station—and has. The power of these tiny machines is incredible; a brisk game of Pac-Man, or a jog around the Visi Calc track, is by no means the limit of their potential.

But there's an irony in all this: when people joke about feeding the dog and taking out the trash, they are instinctively approaching computers the right way.

Computers are best suited to the realm of the mundane and the routine—and they are not to be taken too seriously.

Down

Computers, like boxers and airplanes, go down when they fail. They are also said to crash, or bomb out. The sudden violence implicit in such terms should be taken seriously. This slang originates with hard-core computer technicians. They know what they're talking about.

Drive, Floppy Disk

Think of a disk drive as a precise, high-speed tape deck. Like a tape deck in a hi-fi, it's mechanical, and therefore the most likely component in a computer system to fail. Intermittent disk-drive trouble is an unavoidable part of modern computer life.

Because the computer itself usually works flawlessly, drive trouble is very noticeable. Beginners take it much too seriously when the computer squeaks and complains of an I/O ERROR.

Watch other people using a computer to learn the way they jiggle and fiddle with the disks in the drives.

There's a skill to getting a cranky disk drive to load a program —a mixture of patience and body English. You have to learn it.

Drive, Hard Disk

Hard disk drives are closed boxes the size of ordinary drives. The disks are sealed inside. Because hard drives are sealed, they are untroubled by dust, grime, and the sloppiness of human operators. They are built with much closer tolerances between the drive head and the disk itself. This allows a hard drive to store an enormous amount of information, and to retrieve it rapidly.

Like any piece of precision mechanical equipment, hard drives are expensive—one may cost as much as the computer itself. Nevertheless, hard drives are increasingly common and soon will be standard on all but the smallest, cheapest computers.

Elitism, Computer

Every new technology brings cries of elitism—fears of a ruling "technocracy" controlling the technology, and us. We've heard these cries about film, network television, communication satellites, cable television, home video technology, and, most recently, computers. This clearly demonstrates that people don't understand computers.

Twenty years ago, it was true enough. Computers were huge and expensive, difficult to use, and generally in the possession of large corporations, businesses, and universities, where they were attended by a priestly elite of obscurely educated technicians. In 1963, when I did my college thesis on a computer, I had no direct access to the machine; I never even saw it. I punched my little stack of punch cards, and turned them over to the priests. Some weeks later, I was given a pile of green striped printout. What happened in the interval was a complete mystery; the whole process felt like consulting the oracle at Delphi.

But now this same amount of computing power sits on my desk. I deal with it directly; and I can do any damn thing I please. I can use it to describe the behavior of galaxies or I can use it to make pornographic animated cartoons. It costs as little as a TV set, and a TV is not generally considered an elitist appliance. It can be operated by anyone with a grade-school education, and such education can't be characterized as elitist.

The truth is, small computers aren't elitist at all. On the contrary, they are the first piece of information technology in the twentieth century that breaks the monopolistic hold of large institutions.

Take a hypothetical example. A high-school English teacher has a better way to teach grammar and wants the world to know about it. What are her choices?

If she wrote a textbook, she'd then have to find a publisher; the publisher would demand changes for the market; the resulting book might be distributed well or badly; and so on. If our teacher wanted to make a movie, a television show, or even a video cassette to explain her methods, she'd face still greater restrictions. And these visual media are inherently so expensive that she could not possibly finance the operation on her own.

But if she decided to write a computer program, she could buy a machine for a few hundred dollars, learn programming in a relatively short time, and write her program. And dissemination is a snap—she could put it out on a computer network and it would be immediately available to whoever was interested. Thousands of users around the country could make their own copies of the program cheaply and virtually instantaneously. Some networks would even pay her a royalty.

In fact, this situation is so revolutionary that it is going to create some problems for society as a whole. (See COPYRIGHT.) But by no stretch of the imagination is the new computer technology elitist.

Error Messages

Beginners get a lot of error messages, inevitably accompanied by a sharp electronic beep. Beginners are alarmed by the whole business, jerking their hands from the keyboard as if the machine were about to explode in front of them.

And the messages themselves seem to be the worst sort of reprimand. What is one to make of NEXT WITHOUT FOR ERROR? Or TYPE MISMATCH ERROR? Even if the error message appears to be in English, it's not helpful, such as the self-evident CAN'T CONTINUE ERROR.

The upshot is that beginners don't bother to read error messages. It takes a long time before they realize the machine is helping them find out what's wrong.

Look up error messages in your manual, or press the help buttons on your keyboard. Listen to your machine. It's doing the best it can.

Eyestrain

Sooner or later your eyes will protest against this new demand that they stare at a glowing video screen. You will wonder whether video screens are bad for your eyes.

There is no evidence that they are.

Your eyes will adjust after a while. About the same time that you do.* Especially if you insure good, glare-free lighting and

---

*In England, Her Majesty's Principal Inspector at the Health and Safety Executive, E. A. Cox, concluded, "There are no radiation levels that could be considered to be of concern to the normal individual." American computer consultant Carl Machover has argued that most problems with video screens are psychosomatic in origin: people who feel

proper seating—just as you would when using a typewriter, or watching TV.

Fake

There's a lot of fake computer processing around, and there's going to be more. Just because the printout comes to you with perforated holes on the sides doesn't make it right.

Many programs allow a person to use the computer as a typewriter. Data can be entered with very few internal checks; processing can be modified by human instructions so that it comes out however you want it to come out.

The self-fulfilling prophecy is one of the great psychological truths of human life. Nothing about computers prevents them from verifying that the world is the way you want to believe it is.

In science, where methods of conscious and unconscious data manipulation are well understood, faking information is referred to as "massaging the data," or "fudging results." But it amounts to the same thing.

In the most reprehensible situations, you fool others. In the most destructive situations, you fool yourself.

File

Just like a file in a filing cabinet, a computer file is a collection of related data that is stored and retrieved as a unit. It is helpful to think of files in this physical way. In computer terms, you "open" a file and "read" it; you then "write" in the file, making additions

---

alienated from a new technology will find some way to complain about it. See *New Scientist,* January 27, 1983, p. 229.

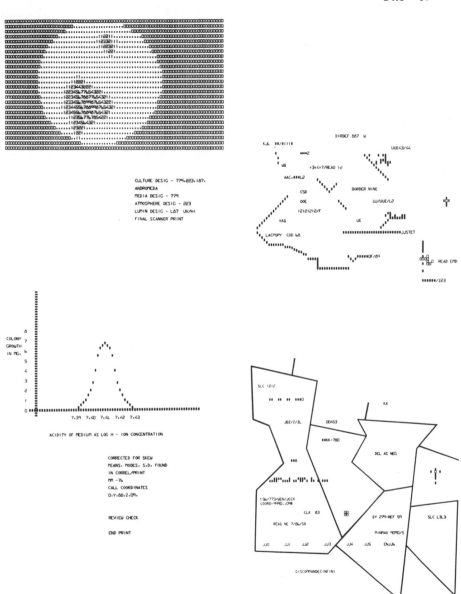

CULTURE DESIG - 779,223,167,
ANDROMEDA
MEDIA DESIG - 779
ATMOSPHERE DESIG - 223
LUMIN DESIG - L67 UV/HI
FINAL SCANNER PRINT

CORRECTED FOR SKEW
MEANS, MODES, S.D. FOUND
IN CORREL/PRINT
MM -76
CALL COORDINATES
0.Y.66.Z.09.

REVIEW CHECK

END PRINT

Examples of fake computer output. Actually, a computer was
not used at all, just an IBM Selectric typewriter with an unusual
typeface.

or changes; and when you are through you "close" the file again. The fact that you are reading and writing from and to a disk makes no real difference.

The significance of the file is exactly what it is in a filing cabinet. How you set up your files determines what you get back, and how easily. There are two big differences.

The first is that the computer can easily handle large files, and can shuffle through the contents of a file rapidly.

The second is that *you* can't shuffle through the file conveniently at all. Browsing is extremely awkward. Computer scientists keep certain kinds of information in regular file cabinets.

They know.

Games

The microcomputer revolution has been spearheaded by games, which is one reason people have such mixed emotions about games.

There are several kinds of games:

1. Arcade games. These are versions of old, mechanical pinball-type games. Within the trade, arcade games are broken down into such subspecies as *invader games,* named for the archetypal Space Invaders; their opposite, the *defender games;* and *eating games,* including Pac-Man and its clones. Because arcade games rely heavily on hand-eye coordination, they're often referred to as *twitch games.* One Atari designer recently remarked that his company had consistently overestimated the intelligence, and underestimated the manual dexterity, of the people who play these games.

2. Strategy games. Chess, backgammon, and other traditional board games, and a generation of newer games that require thinking instead of dexterity, are available on computers.

3. Adventure games. These are new games, a kind of cross between a shaggy-dog story and a complex puzzle, which can only be played on a machine. The player gives commands in English,

such as GO EAST, ENTER THE HOUSE, or TAKE THE KNIFE, as he moves through a fictitious landscape of words and pictures. Adventure games take days or even weeks to play, and manual dexterity is irrelevant.

What is one to think of electronic games? Many individuals and communities express concern about the enormous popularity of arcade games among the young. I'm inclined not to worry.

Arcade games are the hula hoops of the '80s, and already there are indications that the mania for twitch games may be fading. Meanwhile it seems sensible to insist on regular school attendance and some balance between time spent at an arcade hangout and other recreations such as sports.

However, unlike hula hoops, the present generation of computer games represents a transitional phenomenon on the way to a permanent alteration of our world. Computers are the most compelling toy ever invented. Even in the 1950s, games were surreptitiously played on mainframe computers; the first computer video game was invented in 1962. Ever more elaborate and challenging games will be played on computers in the future. Why not? It's a way of making friends with the machine.

Gender, Computers and

Computers have attracted more men than women. In recent years, there have been studies that suggest sex differences in mathematical and linguistic ability—men are more skilled in math, women more skilled in language. But computers are not particularly mathematical, and we may expect both men and women to use them with equal facility.

River Raid, one of the most popular new cartridge games, was designed by a twenty-seven-year-old woman, Carol Shaw. More and more women are using computers on a high programming level.

So if your wife or daughter or secretary or company president tells you she can't understand it, tell her she's a chauvinist.

Generation, Computer

The first personal computer was created by a company called MITS in 1975. It was based on the Intel 8-bit microprocessor. Although that computer, the MITS Altair, is no longer manufactured, it led the first generation of Radio Shack, Apple, and Atari machines in the late 1970s. All first-generation machines were based on 8-bit microprocessors. (A microprocessor is a computer compressed into a single chip. The 8-bit designation indicates how much information the processor can handle at one time, and how much memory it can deal with.)

The second generation of personal computers is based on newer, 16-bit microprocessors. The IBM Personal Computer was the first popular 16-bit machine; more than twenty different 16-bit computers are now being sold. These machines work faster, have more memory, and cost more than 8-bit machines. They also have fewer programs and attachments available.

In a couple of years, there will be a generation of 32-bit machines available. And so the cycle will continue, into the indefinite future.

This creates a consumer dilemma. Each time a new generation of machines is introduced, the market is chaotic, the machines are unproven, and they have few programs available. After three or four years, there is more reliability and there are more programs, but the machines that run them are increasingly old-fashioned.

The solution for home users and first-time purchasers is to buy late in the cycle. A proven machine with a large stock of programs will be far more satisfactory than a hot new machine with nothing to run on it. The Apple II has 16,000 programs available; the Atari 800 has 2,000. The IBM PC has 1,000. Some of the newer machines have only three or four.

Pay your money; take your choice.

Hands-on Experience

You can't get comfortable with computers by talking about them or by reading books, including this one. You need hands-on, direct experience.

Learning to run a computer is like learning to deliver a tennis serve, to cook a soufflé, or to drive a car.

You have to get out there and do it.

Hardware

If you can touch it, it's hardware. That's simple enough. All the trouble arises from the supposedly opposite term, software. (See SOFTWARE.)

Heat

Computers don't tolerate excessive heat. If your machine works fine when you first turn it on, but begins to behave erratically after an hour or two, you may need an air-conditioned room, or a fan attachment for your machine, or both.

Help!

The best source of help is another person: a friend with a machine like yours, the neighbor's kid, a salesman. It will make your life much easier, when you start to use a program, if you can arrange telephone access to some person who already knows the program.

The next best source of help is printed information: documentation on the machine or the program, or a book. Most of your questions are answered somewhere in the documentation.

The worst source is the telephone number of the manufacturer of the program or the machine. This number, somewhere in northern California, is always busy.

Many machines and programs now come with built-in help menus and buttons. These may or may not actually help.

Hurting the Computer

Many beginners worry that they may do something that will hurt the machine.

Short of drop-kicking it or soaking it in the bathtub, there's not much you can do to hurt the machine. That shouldn't be a concern.

However, there are plenty of ways to lose your data, which is why you should back up your disks and treat them gently.

Information, Computers and

It's disquieting to hear that computers will provide us with more information. Perhaps you feel you're already bombarded with too much information.

But what people really intend when they speak of information is meaning, not facts. Undoubtedly we're bombarded with too many facts—isolated bits of data without context. You may read in the newspaper that "two feet of snow fell in Milwaukee last month." That's a fact: but what does it mean? Is two feet a lot or a little? Did it cause some particular disruption? Did it all fall in a single storm, or six inches a week? What's the point of mentioning this fact?

To assign meaning always requires more information to organize what we have. And it is this organization that computers have a talent for. Computers can take large numbers of facts and convert them into comparisons, spreadsheets, graphs. In short, they can help us to assign meanings.

More meaning, and fewer facts.

That's the idea, anyway.

The information-handling facility of computers will force us to learn general techniques to assess information. This is long overdue in any case.

Foremost among these techniques is the branch of mathematics known as statistics. It's extraordinary how many educated people lack even the most rudimentary comprehension of statistics. Most understand that statistics is a formal way to arrange information according to means, standard deviations, averages, and so forth.

But the real importance of statistics lies in its power to evaluate information. If there were ten nuclear accidents last year and thirteen this year, does this prove that nuclear accidents are on the rise? It may not. In the most literal sense, the facts don't speak for themselves.

Yet most discussions of facts, even high-level discussions, proceed from the assumption that the only way to challenge conclusions is to challenge the raw data from which the conclusions are drawn. Such challenges are highly emotional, since they derive from the old—and incorrect—belief that figures don't lie but liars figure. Yet without statistical evaluation, figures do lie. They lie all the time.

Statistics represents an impersonal method for assessing the credibility of both raw data and the conclusions drawn from that data. Its use can save a lot of shouting, and a lot of hot air.

The fact that the practice of sophisticated statistical analysis is not more widely used may mean that it's a little like more efficient tax enforcement—nobody really wants it. One can argue that certain disputes are better resolved by shouting than by rational thought. Furthermore, since statistics is mathematical, it is frequently counter-intuitive in its results. That's another reason people don't like it. A final reason is that statistics often tell you that nothing is going on—or that something is going on—when you'd prefer to believe the reverse.

Input

Whatever is put into the computer. Widely used in ordinary conversation, as in "Give me your input." This usage began with engineers and computer people, and is now omnipresent. Everybody's giving his input to everybody else.

My input is that I oppose machine terms for human actions. If you mean "Tell me what you think," then say that. You might just be rewarded with some thinking, instead of some input.

Intelligence, Artificial

I want to make four points about the thirty-year-old study of artificial intelligence, or AI.

1. *There is no theoretical limit to what machines can do.* No aspect of human behavior is so unique or special that machines cannot perform the same function—or appear to do so. The world backgammon champion is a machine. Computer chess programs

whip all but the most gifted human opponents. Computers can diagnose disease as skillfully as human physicians can in certain instances. These are all activities earlier observers insisted "a computer can never do."

You'd think by now everyone would have gotten the point: there is nothing a machine can't do.

2. *The machine isn't doing it the way we do it.* Depending on your point of view, this fact is either deeply troubling or irrelevant. But certainly it suggests a danger that naïve computer users will attribute to the machines qualities they do not really possess.

3. *Getting the machine to do it is hard.* Genuine artificial intelligence has been a long time coming. In fact, it's quite a bit overdue. In the 1960s, most AI researchers were predicting true artificial intelligence within thirty years. As recently as 1975, a few observers still expected it within ten years. Now some AI workers are saying that real artificial intelligence is a hundred to three hundred years away.

Yet limited examples of artificial intelligence are not so far off. Certainly in the next decade there will be "expert systems" highly skilled in specialized areas such as medicine, law, or engineering. These expert systems may be so adept that it will be difficult for professionals to ignore the advice of the machine in many instances.

But the general-purpose artificial intelligence, the machine that will make your coffee, commiserate with you over your automobile accident and sue whoever hit you, do your laundry, check your sore throat, and advise you on your career angst, is not hovering in the wings.

4. *AI is a branch of human psychology.* This conclusion is not self-evident, although it should be. Artificial intelligence is really focused on how human beings do various tasks. This is only natural, since before you can instruct a machine to imitate human actions, you need to understand what human actions really are.

The quest for artificial intelligence has provoked intense scrutiny of the most obvious and therefore unexamined components of human behavior: how you recognize a friend, how you tell whether the friend is happy or sad, how you decide what to say to your friend, and so on. This is a very different order of problem from how to solve a quadratic equation, or even how to translate Russian into English.

Marvin Minsky, an artificial-intelligence pioneer, observes that it's often easy to make machines do things that are hard for people, and hard to make machines do things that are often easy for people. A decade ago, Minsky's laboratory at MIT tried to make a machine that could play Ping-Pong. The lab encountered severe problems in attempting to duplicate this human pastime.

In any event, it is easy to be distracted by the artificial part of artificial intelligence. At the moment, the limitations of AI are the limitations of human psychology, not the limitations of computers. AI will thus remain a field of study devoted to understanding human behavior—at least for the foreseeable future.

I/O

The common abbreviation I/O means Input/Output. It's a subject of considerable importance to users. The way a computer gets its information (input), and the way it responds (output), is the principal determinant of how the machine feels to a user. Input/Output is the equivalent of how an automobile "handles."

Most computer users find that they wish for a little more understanding—in all senses of the word—from their machines. They dream of more "natural" kinds of interaction. A good deal of current effort is directed toward that goal. It takes two forms: mechanical devices, and programs.

Information is usually entered on a panel of keys. The keyboard is such a familiar device that we do not stop to think how arbitrary it is. The keyboard was invented in 1867, shortly after the Civil War. Its present form was pretty well fixed by about 1875. Few things have persisted unchanged from that time. This makes the keyboard rather like a clam—a simple creature that hasn't evolved much over a great span of time.

When the computer was first widely used, in the 1950s, it was in effect inserted into the middle of the familiar typewriter. The typewriter keyboard was on one side—the input side—and the paper roller and striking keys were on the other side—the output side. Later, another familiar device, the television, was hooked up to the computer along with the typewriter.

This pattern of handling input and output with machinery adapted from other areas was established during the earliest days of computers. Over the forty-year history of these machines, surprisingly few devices have been invented specifically for interacting with the computer. To be sure, there are graphics tablets, joysticks, light pens, optical character-recognition devices, and so-called mice that control cursors. Yet most users still interact through the familiar keyboard, monitor, and printer.

The next ten years should see a proliferation of new devices. Touch-sensitive screens will be widely used. Machines that speak in limited ways are already common, and machines that accept spoken input will become more common. Within twenty years, optical devices will allow machines to recognize faces and previously seen objects. In fact, a range of sensory devices should give machines the ability to touch, smell, hear, and see. And computers will certainly become more mobile after 1990.

Less spectacular developments will affect the keyboard, monitor, and printer. Keyboard design is long overdue for change. (See KEYBOARD.) Monitor screens will be thin, and will display high-resolution lettering in a greater variety of sizes and typefaces defined by user-controlled character generators. Printers will be quieter and faster, and will routinely print in color. Buffer memories for peripherals will increase in size. For example, there is talk of building memory into monitors, so that you could load text into your thin screen, unplug the screen from the computer, and go sit on the couch to read, as you now read a book.

These mechanical changes will alter the way we feel about computers, as well as the way we interact with them. But they are less important than changes in programming sophistication.

. . .

Why can't you talk to a computer in ordinary English? Why can't it compensate for little mistakes? Why can't it know what you mean?

In short, why can't a computer be more like a man?

There are two answers. The first concerns hardware. Since computers operate as a series of on/off switches, all high-level languages must translate specific commands into specific switching instructions. This requires memory. The more commands you build into the language, and the more flexible you make the grammar, the more machine memory you require.

For most of computer history, memory has been expensive. Scientists designed languages that would not take up so much memory that none was left to do any computing work; there was no point in creating a flexible machine that understood everything but could do nothing about it.

But memory has become ever more available and cheap. Desk-top computers will have usable memories of a thousand kilobytes or more in the next year, or two hundred times what is now built into desk-top machines. Large, inexpensive memory eliminates the hardware barrier to creating machines that understand ordinary language.

But what remains is the second, more difficult problem of creating a program that instructs the machine to understand so-called natural language.

It's not easy. Anyone who has tried to explain a joke to someone who speaks another language knows that languages are laden with cultural assumptions, non-literal meanings, and ambiguities. For example, how would you explain these sentences:

"Time flies when you're having a good time."
"I'll tell you in my good time."
"I played a game of tennis in my time."
"I play tennis all the time."
"Let's play one more time."
"Let's play another time."
"I play when I get time."
"I got to the court in time."

"I got to the court on time."
"My timing was good."
"There isn't time for tennis."
"This isn't the time for tennis."
"Can you tell me the time?"
"Can you tell time?"
"Time will tell."

If you were obliged to teach someone the formal rules for these sentences, you'd spend a lot of time at it. It's not surprising that understanding natural languages has eluded programmers for decades. It'll be a while before you greet your machine with "Good morning. Turn yourself on and let's get going."

However, simpler interactions are possible. Already so-called front-end expert systems enable the user to interact with the machine in ordinary, if somewhat restricted, English. Essentially, front-end systems are AI programs interposed between the keyboard and the stored data. Like a false façade on an old building, what you now see is the new surface, not the old bricks. The front-end program allows you to interact with a certain degree of informality and imprecision; these programs seem to "know what you mean." They require a lot of memory and a lot of computing power, and probably will not be available for home machines until 32-bit computers are common.

But even before then, we'll see a great increase in machine tolerance for human error. If you type PPRINT, the machine can easily scan an internal vocabulary, find the closest match, and respond, I THINK YOU MEANT *PRINT*. IS THAT CORRECT? If you agree, the machine will fix the error for you. Certainly the days when any computer responds with a cryptic SYNTAX ERROR are numbered.

Furthermore, there is no reason why the machine cannot begin to "know" your quirks. If you consistently make some error (I frequently type FREUQENTLY, LSIT for LIST, and THJE for THE), the machine can begin to compensate for you without asking. Some computers already do this in a primitive way.

If these tendencies are extended, it is possible for a computer to "figure out what you are trying to do" on a higher level. That is, despite errors in several statements, the machine could scan the overall structure of the instructions, detect the pattern, and respond: I THINK I UNDERSTAND WHAT YOU MEAN. YOU WANT TO MAKE A TABLE OF VALUES OF 8 MULTIPLIED BY EVERY NUMBER FROM 1 TO 20. IS THAT CORRECT?

Such instruction scanning is far simpler than genuine language comprehension, but it would make computers more lifelike and easy to use. Experimental programs already perform far more sophisticated text analyses.

It's important to note that every development discussed so far is purely mechanical. A computer that corrects your errors may seem more intelligent, but it's just a more sophisticated mechanical device. It's demonstrable that what most people define as mechanical is merely repetitive. It's easy to get rid of that repetitive quality, by programming multiple statements of equivalent error messages—having the machine first say, for example:

I THINK I UNDERSTAND WHAT YOU MEAN.
LET ME SEE IF I UNDERSTAND YOUR MEANING.
DO YOU MEAN THE FOLLOWING?

This gives a more "alive" quality to the machine, but you shouldn't be fooled. It's still just a machine.

Jargon

All this talk of RAM and ROM, bits and bytes, CP/M and DBM, single and double density, buffers and peripherals . . . It's enough to drive anyone away whimpering.

But cooks don't think twice about the extensive vocabulary of the kitchen. Sports fans wield a vast jargon; incredible specialized knowledge is needed to follow a football game. Everybody knows at least fifty terms for automobile anatomy. An ordinary·home stereo has at least forty specialized terms,* most of

---

*Receiver, tuner, amplifier, turntable, tape deck, speaker, watts, ohms, jack, headphones, connector, cartridge, needle, arm, AM, FM, Dolby, LED, phonograph, volume,

them printed on the outside controls, but nobody's put off by stereos.

Of course, we've had years to assimilate all this. And we've forgotten that thirty years ago, when "hi-fi" was new, most people were dismayed by the specialized new terminology.

Computer jargon is neither extensive nor forbidding. It's just new, and it takes time. After a few months, new computer users find themselves chattering away happily about RAM and ROM— and it actually means something to them!

Jobs

Worried about losing your job to a machine? Most people are. Are your worries justified? That's hard to say.

It should be clear by now that nobody really understands how an industrial economy works. If anybody did, we wouldn't have problems keeping it running smoothly.

Similarly, there's no satisfactory way to think about what happens with the arrival of automation, except to say that it's not news when a company offers a thousand new jobs, or when certain industries haven't been able to get enough people for years—but ouster by a goddamn robot is widely and emotionally reported.

I have trouble with the doomsayers who foresee human beings on the soup lines and machines ladling out the soup. Nor am I persuaded by the image of everyone tripping through sunlit fields like characters from *Elvira Madigan* while machines do all the work and create all the wealth for us.

My guess is that:
1. Everyone will work differently.
2. Everyone will work less.

---

input, loudness, balance, bass, treble, mono, stereo, mute, record, pause, rewind, play, monitor, selector, auxiliary, timer, counter, rewind, fast forward, ground.

3. Everyone will work who wants to work.
But that's only a guess.

Keyboard

The standard typewriter keyboard, the so-called QWERTY keyboard, was first made shortly after the American Civil War. Originally, the need to prevent jamming of the keys determined the arrangement of the letters. In essence, our keyboard was designed to slow typing down.

With the advent of electric typewriters, mechanical limitations became unimportant, and new keyboards were invented. One was laid out by August Dvorak, who studied which keys were actually most often pressed. The Dvorak keyboard moved most of the typing to the right hand (the QWERTY board has almost 60 percent of typing done by the left hand), and in general reduced the amount of jumping around the hands have to do. Even more radical keyboards have been invented, notably the PCD-Maltron, a sculptured board that looks as if it melted somewhere along the line.

But all new keyboards have faced the same resistance—nobody wants to learn a non-standard keyboard; no one wants to learn typing twice; no office wants to install new boards and have to retrain everybody.

Computers change all this. Many computers have plug-in keyboards, and the computer doesn't care what arrangement the keyboard has; it merely needs to be told which key, when pressed, stands for which letter. Different keyboards can be used by different operators on the same machine—and will be.

This will enable you to overcome minor design irritations. When IBM built its Personal Computer, it abandoned the keyboard layout of the IBM Selectric typewriter, even though the 9 million IBM Selectrics already sold have made the Selectric keyboard an office standard. Why IBM changed its computer keyboard is a mystery, particularly since the new keyboard is in many respects not an improvement.

But increasingly the rule of computers is: if you don't like it, you can change it. As a matter of fact, you can even design your own keyboard, reassigning the keys in whatever way you like. Many users have.

Three terms:

Monopanel or membrane keyboards are single sheets of plastic with touch-sensitive areas. Monopanel keyboards appear on cheaper computers and limit them severely, since you cannot rest your fingers on the keys.

Expanded keyboards are QWERTY keyboards with extra keys for entering numerical data, or for program control.

Soft keys are user-definable. This means that you can tell the computer what you want a key to mean, and the computer will accept your instructions.

Languages, Computer

Computers carry out their work through thousands of on/off switches. In mathematical terms they use binary notation, a series of 1's and 0's. This is efficient for a computer but awkward for people. (A few people can program in direct binary notation but that's beyond most of us.)

To make machine interaction easier for people, computer languages have been developed. A language is a code for talking to a machine. If I want to print out some information, I'd like to tell the machine to WRITE or PRINT it. But machines don't understand WRITE or PRINT; they only understand 1's and 0's. So the code must be provided to the machine, so that it knows what WRITE or PRINT or GET or SAVE means in its own electrical terms. The code can be wired into the machine, or it can be entered as programs. But the machine must be given the language before I can start talking to it.

There are hundreds of computer languages, each with advantages and disadvantages, advocates and detractors. But computer languages are all pretty similar. They each have a "vocabulary" of about a hundred reserved words; they each have a rigid grammar; they each can be learned in from ten to forty hours. It's easy to go from one language to another, and a professional programmer will know several.

If you're thinking of learning a language, which should you learn? Three languages were especially designed for beginners— BASIC, Pascal, and Logo.

All personal computers come with some version of BASIC, a language developed in the late 1960s by John Kemeny and Thomas Kurtz at Dartmouth College. For better or worse—some say for worse—BASIC is the most common small-computer language.

Complaints about the appropriateness of BASIC focus on the "unstructured" quality of the language. Newer languages force organization on you, and assist you to think more clearly. Pascal, developed in 1970 by the Swiss computer scientist Niklaus Wirth, is such a language. The most common version is UCSD Pascal, developed at the University of California, San Diego, by Kenneth L. Bowles. A still newer language, Logo, was defined by Seymour Papert and his co-workers at MIT in the 1970s.

Then which should you learn? Experts engage in violent disputes, but for the average person it isn't really a problem. If you just want to dabble, or to write short programs of less than a page to customize purchased programs—say, to make your printer do something special—then BASIC is the quickest to learn and the easiest to use. And it really is the *lingua franca* of small computers; all computers speak BASIC, and most magazine articles are written in it. On the other hand, if you want to get serious and write long programs, you'll be much happier with Pascal. For children, Logo is best.

All the languages mentioned are *high-level languages.* They are closer to English than binary numbers. But there is something more primitive, called *assembly language.* Assembly language is close to direct binary machine code, and uses abbreviations such as **JMP** and **INY** for single-step commands. It's not for beginners.*

Learning

There are reasons to think that all forms of learning are similar. It's easier to think about learning in a physical context than in an intellectual context. If you're learning a tennis backhand or a golf swing, the first rule is *slow down.* Do the action in slow motion, feel the different stages.

The next rule is *tolerate your own errors.* You're going to hit a few balls wildly, particularly at first. Suspend self-criticism.

The third rule is *learn by direct experience.* Reading a book on tennis strokes has limited value. The same is true of computers. Unless the machine is in front of you, and you're typing as you read, the exercise has limited value.

The fourth rule is *learn by example.* Often you can simply imitate a teacher and get the hang of it. The same is true of computers. I'm not opposed to typing in programs even if you don't understand them. You'll start to learn, if only by fixing your typing errors.

The final rule is *work at short intervals.* Nobody takes a five-hour tennis lesson. Learning a computer can't be done in long stretches either.

---

*Minsky notes that specialists use it when they want to get the greatest possible speed from the computer—and the least possible speed from the programmer.

Literacy, Computer

This unfortunate term has been adopted for everything from knowing computer jargon to the practical ability to run these machines. It's unfortunate because it suggests all kinds of wrong ideas.

"Literacy" has two meanings. The first is the ability to read and write a language, in this case presumably a computer language. Yet the majority of computer users operate their machines quite happily without any programming ability at all—just as most car owners drive without knowledge of auto mechanics.

Furthermore, if one learns a computer language, writing for a machine involves a process utterly different from, say, writing an essay in Italian or French. No one sits down and writes a computer program, hands it to the machine, and walks away. Computers display such finicky precision that even short programs must be tested line by line. Writing a program is thus interactive with the machine, and has the quality of a struggle, trying to make the damned thing understand.

Therefore, when used in this sense, computer literacy involves not only what words to say to the machine, but also *how* to say them. "Computer competence" would be a much better term.

The second meaning for literacy is the state of being informed or educated about a subject. To the extent that "computer literacy" means simply knowing something about computers, it's a waste of time. These days, if you can't actually use the machines, you're in trouble—because you're computer incompetent, no matter how computer literate you may think you are.

Literacy, Ordinary

One unrecognized change of the Computer Age is the revived emphasis on plain old literacy.

For a while there, when we were in the Television Age, it seemed as though information were going to be increasingly visual, and people wouldn't have to bother anymore with old-fashioned language and linear thinking. Illiteracy was going to be okay. You'd just see some product on TV, and go out and find it in the supermarket by recognizing the colors on the box.

Well, now the Computer Age is here and linear thinking is required—with a vengeance. The computer is the most fiercely linear invention imaginable. And it requires the ability to read and write.

Actually, illiteracy was never a good idea unless you aspired to be a slave. Knowledge is power, and knowledge exists as manipulated symbols. That's been true for several thousand years. It isn't going to change anytime soon.

Machines and Men

We are entering a period when it will be important to distinguish clearly between what men can do and what machines can do. Unfortunately the distinction has been blurred in recent years.

The astronauts are the most publicized example of men turned into machines. When the first astronauts landed on the moon, the world cheered—but with reservations, for it was clear that these "men" behaved in rather inhuman ways. The first man on the moon should have shouted "Gosh! I'm standing on the moon!" But he didn't. There weren't a lot of spontaneous yucks from the Apollo astronauts, and for very good reasons. They had been living in simulators for months on end, grinding the humanness out of them; they were totally dedicated to "the mission," and perceived themselves as integrated with the "onboard mission systems." They were aware that their every heartbeat and breath was monitored and measured, watched from Earth like any other mechanical system on the spacecraft that might fail.

Yet the latter twentieth century has been influenced by NASA in ways more subtle than Teflon pots and pans. To the extent that people agree with Chris Krafft, head of the Johnson Space Center, that astronauts "represent the cream of the crop of human beings," machine-like human behavior may be perceived as acceptable, and even desirable. It's not surprising that we've begun to apply machine terms to describe ordinary human behavior. People are "wired," "turned on," and "plugged in"; people give their "input" and produce their "output"; people no longer decide, they "exercise a decision-making function."*

Similarly, machines are attributed qualities appropriate only to people. In casual conversation, a computer program may be said "to behave like," "to believe itself to be," or "to act as if it thinks it is" something or other. Such expressions are usually intended to be amusing or ironic. But naïve minds may accept them as literal truth, and repetition always produces reinforcement, however unconsciously.

To say that a program "believes" anything at all is as fundamental an error as to say that a person is "turned on" by anything at all. Human beings are not provoked to action in the same way as a stereo amplifier. Not even by analogy.

We risk loss of humanity whenever we treat a man as a machine. Fortunately, men usually can't live up to their machine conception. Even the astronauts had the good grace to throw up occasionally, or get the flu, or do something else that differentiated them from the machinery aboard the spacecraft.

But the reverse is not always true. A sophisticated computer may not provide clear signals that it is only a machine. Its machine

---

*This criticism shouldn't be pushed too far; at bottom, nothing new is happening. It's demonstrable that human emotions are inexpressible except by analogy; people have undoubtedly "burned" with desire and "glowed" with excitement ever since they huddled around cave fires.

nature may be difficult to recognize; it is up to us to keep the mechanical truth firmly in mind.

Twenty years ago, Arthur C. Clarke listed the differences between a camera and the human eye, concluding that the human eye was inferior to the camera. Clarke is a wonderfully intelligent observer of man and science, but his point can be just as easily turned upside down. It's simple to show that the human eye is vastly superior to any camera if one includes the film as well as the camera itself. The human eye registers an image that no camera can duplicate, because the visible light exposure range of the human eye exceeds that of any film stock by at least a factor of 10.* The very sharpness of man-made lenses is problematical in many situations because it is so unnatural. Much effort in photography is devoted to decreasing lens sharpness.

One eventually concludes that the camera is neither better nor worse than the human eye, only different. And the difference—the difference between what is human and what is machine—is something we must never forget.

We are not machines, and machines are not people. Not now, and not for a long time to come. Personally, I think not ever, although at the far reaches of imagination this becomes an issue of philosophy.

But as a practical, immediate consideration, no philosophical issue is involved. People are people. Machines are machines. Only a fool confuses them.

Magnetic Fields

Strong magnetic fields erase floppy disks. You've probably never cared whether or not objects in your working environment create a magnetic field, but you'll have to pay attention now.

Telephones create a field whenever they ring; don't put a disk

---

*This situation finally changed in 1982, with the introduction of Eastman 5293 film stock, which uses two separate emulsions to record a great exposure range.

next to a phone. Television sets create fields; if you stack disks on top of a TV, you're asking for trouble. All stereo equipment is suspect. My lovely high-tech Italian desk lamp has a transformer built into the base; it creates a magnetic field when it's on. Scissors and screwdrivers may be magnetized. Electrical motors in clocks and toys create fields. Some wristwatches create fields. Any unshielded electrical cord creates a field around it.

These facts should make you careful but not crazy. After all, magnetic fields diminish rapidly with distance; you can place your disks six inches from the telephone without worry. But you never know what will happen. Even if everyone in your office is mindful of magnetic fields, the night cleaning crew or the weekend repairman may not be. Protect yourself: don't leave your disks lying around, and keep backup copies in a safe place.

Mathematics

Computers have little to do with mathematics these days. Even the experience of programming in a high-level language is not particularly mathematical. It's much more like talking to a cranky aunt who doesn't hear well. You say, "I've just been outside," and she replies, "I never told you to hide." *That's* what programming is like.

Memory

We are not accustomed to dealing with machines with memories. The very idea of machine memory, and the associated jargon, gives beginners trouble.

To begin with, there are three kinds of memory.

Random Access Memory, or RAM, is memory that is available

to the user. Think of RAM as lots of little cubbyholes in the computer, each capable of storing a single number or letter of the alphabet. Small computers have from 16K to 256K of RAM, meaning they have 16,000 to 256,000 cubbyholes.

RAM is temporary memory. You get to fill those cubbyholes up, but whatever you put into them will be stored only as long as the power is on. If the electricity goes, all the information in RAM goes, too.

Disks can hold information, too. A single side of a 5¼-inch floppy disk will hold at least 140K—equivalent to about 70 typewritten pages. Thus, in most computer systems the disk holds far more information than will fit into the computer memory at a single time.

The computer communicates with the disk; information can be swapped back and forth between the disk and the memory. Beginners are invariably confused about where information is in the system—is it on the disk, or in memory, or both? The distinction is important, because if power is turned off, information on the disk is preserved but information in memory is lost.

A friend of mine spent all one Saturday afternoon entering accounts for his small business. After three hours, the house lights flickered briefly—and he had to start all over. He didn't realize that simply entering data from the keyboard doesn't preserve it.

The trouble is that once entered, the data *looks* quite permanent. You can move through it, manipulate it, push it and pull it like taffy. It's difficult to accept that it's only temporarily there.

Most programs allow you to save your data quickly on the disk at the press of a key, and keep right on going where you left off. Experienced users do this every fifteen minutes or so. That way, if the power dies, you only lose the last fifteen minutes of work.

It also gets you into the habit of frequently saving work. It's extremely common for someone to get lost in his work, do a satisfying few hours, pat himself on the back, and flick the machine off—only to realize he forgot to save his work at the end of the session.

Another friend powered up her machine and loaded in a couple of chapters of her new novel from the disk. She was just beginning to work when the power went out. The information was gone. She spent the next hour tearing her hair out over the loss of her precious chapters. Finally, she sat down to rewrite it—and discovered that it was still on the disk. All that torn hair for nothing. The information was safe all along.

Thus a beginner must proceed carefully for a while, until you develop a "feel" for where information is.

Two ideas seem to be troublesome:

First, although disk and memory can communicate, they're separate. You must instruct them to communicate. They don't do it automatically.

And second, when you load or save information on a disk, you're copying it, not transferring it. Beginners think that when the information is loaded from the disk to memory, it is somehow removed from the disk and placed in memory. It's not. The loaded information is still on the disk. Similarly, when you save information to the disk from memory, it is still retained in memory. You've just copied the memory onto the disk.

The interaction of memory and disk is like Xeroxing, not like mailing.

The second kind of machine memory is ROM, or Read-Only Memory. ROM is memory that has been permanently filled: cubbyholes stuffed with letters and then sealed in the factory. It's confusing to call ROM a form of memory at all, since it's so different from RAM. You can't use ROM for your programs, and losing electrical power will not destroy information in ROM.

Read-Only Memory exists only for the use of the machine. ROM contains internal administrative programs such as languages and operating systems. Since ROM is for the machine only, I recommend that you forget about it. Only the rank novice announces proudly, "I've got 40K of ROM!"

The third kind of memory is buffer memory. It's a special variety of RAM. Buffers exist between the main memory and the disk, and sometimes between the main memory and the printer or some other peripheral device. You can dump the contents of the main memory into the buffer, and then the printer will print out whatever is in the buffer, freeing you to continue working on new information in the main memory.

Most users end up wanting more Random Access Memory. The history of small computers has been characterized by increasing amounts of RAM. The earliest machines had only 4K; most machines are now sold with at least 16K, and many users feel unhappy without at least 64K. What's it all for?

In the first place, the machines rarely allow the user all the RAM. Besides their own ROM, computers frequently eat into RAM for such tasks as running the disk drives, handling additional languages, or connecting to peripheral equipment. A disk drive may consume 10K of RAM; a language interpreter another 10K. A page of graphics may require 8K, and animation 16K. At this rate, 64K of RAM disappears fast.

Furthermore, as users become accustomed to their machines, they begin to want simultaneous processing. When you start using a word processor, you find it's a wonderful time-saver. But after you've typed in your text, you must wait while the machine checks spelling. Then you must wait while it prints out your pages. You forget that the whole procedure is many times faster than you could ever do it before. All this waiting around for the machine gets on your nerves. You start to wonder why the machine can't simultaneously check spelling and print out while you keep typing.

Or if you're working with graphics, you wonder why you can't have more detailed images, in more colors, drawn faster. If you're programming, you want more English-like languages.

Whatever the reason, you end up wanting more memory. And machines with 512K to 1,000K of RAM will be commonplace by the mid-1980s.

Microchip

If you remove the cover from any desk-top computer, you will see a green plastic board with lots of tiny black rectangles plugged into it. These black rectangles are microchips.

Each chip has a different function. The largest one is probably the microprocessor—the chip that does the actual computing work. Surrounding chips add memory, provide languages, run the disk drives, and so on. Microchips are identified by the code numbers stamped on them. Some chips are standard parts employed in many computers. Other chips are specially manufactured for a particular computer.

The design of the computer, its so-called architecture, is determined by the way the various microchips are linked together. You're looking at the architecture on a gross level.

Actually, the black rectangles are not the microchips themselves, but a plastic or ceramic covering. If you were to break open one of these coverings, you'd find inside a little silvery flake of silicon, a third of the size of the black rectangle. This is the actual chip. Dozens of fine wires run out from the chip to the prongs that plug the chip into the green board.

You'd need a powerful microscope to see that the silvery surface of the chip is etched in complex patterns. These patterns allow the chip to perform the function of thousands and thousands of electronic components.

Thus, when you remove the cover of a computer, you actually see the equivalent of an aerial view of a city—you can see the basic layout of streets and buildings, but the real level of everyday hustle and bustle occurs on far too small a scale to see.

Microprocessors, or How I Flunked Biostatistics at Harvard

In 1967, all students at the Harvard Medical School were required to take a biostatistics course. At this time there was a newly emergent class of specialist, called a biostatistician, who was consulted by working biologists with the same frequency that Mafia hit men consult their lawyers, and for the same reason—to ask, "Can I get away with this? Is my work unobjectionable?"

Thus, in 1967, to teach biostatistics to every medical student had its revolutionary aspect; the idea was to make all young doctors self-sufficient to carry out their own statistical analyses, and to evaluate those of others. It was imagined we would read every journal article critically, and then sit down with pencil and paper to scratch out the calculations and determine if the authors had done their sums correctly or not.

But this focus on self-reliance (and a rather prissy instructor) led to a final examination where we were expected to calculate standard deviations *by hand.* And the calculation of standard deviations requires the calculation of *square roots* by hand.

I'd done a lot of statistical work before medical school, and although I set up the formulas on paper for my final, I flatly refused to do these calculations by hand. Desk-top calculators were available for such drudgery; every lab had them. I pointed this out.

And I went further. I predicted that within ten years there would be calculators the size of a pack of cigarettes, and costing only a hundred dollars. Thus, I argued, there was no need to bother doing square roots by hand, since it was a virtually obsolete skill.

For this bit of prediction, I got a sarcastic note in red pencil, and a D grade. My instructor took pains to remind me that desk-top calculators in 1967 were larger than a typewriter, weighed more than thirty pounds, and cost several hundred dollars. My instructor disagreed that they would ever become as small and as cheap as I claimed in my lifetime, let alone in ten years. He made some further nasty remarks about my propensity for science fiction, and underlined the D grade twice, emphatically.

Texas Instruments sold the first pocket calculators in 1971.

Unfortunately, by that time I was two years out of medical school, and in no position to deliver the stinging rebuttal my instructor had richly earned.

But the point of this story is not to demonstrate that I was right and he was wrong. To tell the truth, I had grave doubts about my prediction (almost as grave as the doubts about my ability to do square roots by hand). Although I felt certain that pocket-size miniaturization could be achieved within ten years, I was not at all convinced about the hundred-dollar price tag. Such a cheap price implied volume sales. And after all, a miniature calculator capable of carrying out square roots was a pretty specialized item, like a spectrometer or an amino acid analyzer. It might be useful to a few laboratories, but who else would want one?

The man on the street had no earthly use for a miniature calculator. What would he want one for? Balancing his checkbook? You didn't need to carry something in your pocket to do that. And after he balanced his checkbook, then what? I could think of no other use.

I still can't.

But these days, everybody seems to carry a calculator. Women have them in their purses like perfume spray. Men have them in their wallets and built into their watches. Kids take them to school. (*That* at least makes sense.) Yet I never see anybody using them. I don't know what they carry them around for. I carry one, too, and I don't know why. Once every couple of months, I use it, but I never do anything with it that I couldn't do by hand.

But the real point is that the whole society seems to have decided *en masse* that it wants calculators. Everybody must have a calculator to feel equipped to face the day. And this consensus has been reached in the same mysterious way that previous consumer decisions have been made against the SST, in favor of television, against eight-track cassettes, in favor of FM stereo, against quadraphonic sound, in favor of videotape, against the laser disk, and so on.

My prediction failed to anticipate that everybody and his grandmother would want this specialized item. And it failed in another aspect as well—I did not anticipate the invention of the microprocessor, the computer on a chip.

I wasn't the only one.

What happened was a curious event. In 1970, a Japanese firm asked Intel, a leading microchip company, to create a whole series of different chips for an intended line of small calculators. An engineer at Intel named Ted Hoff argued that the most efficient procedure would be to create a single microprocessor chip, which could then be modified in its functions with specialized peripheral chips. This was done: and the Intel microprocessor chip began the small-computer era.

Mindless Machines, the Virtues of

Consider for a moment the differences between talking to a computer and talking to another human being. Human communication occurs on many levels simultaneously: the literal meaning of the words we speak, the tone of voice they are spoken in, the rhythms and accents. We also observe facial expressions, bodily movement, dress, grooming, and so on. Smell and touch may be important in some situations.

Furthermore, we have a memory for prior communications with a particular person, allowing us to compare the present interaction with past ones. Finally, we may bring outside knowledge to the interaction; if we know George was just fired from his job, we expect communication with him to take certain forms. And so on.

In contrast to the incredibly rich quality of human communication, computer interaction is thin and literal-minded. The computer accepts information on a single channel only—generally keys pressed at a keyboard. And it only accepts literal information: if you're upset and making an unusually large number of typos today, the machine won't notice. Although some computer systems require a password or other identification, they can't be said to "know" you, or to remember past interactions with you, any more than your house knows you because you have a key to the front door.

Because the machine is so literal-minded, it makes no allowances within the single channel of communication. If you type PPRINT "THIS IS A SENTENCE," the computer won't guess that you meant to type PRINT. It'll simply quit working. In fact, it won't compensate in any way for you. An architect's draftsman knows what kind of building he is drawing, and can correct minor errors depending on whether it's a skyscraper or a family dwelling. A computer draftsman just cranks it out, mistakes and all, in a way that we would call "mindless."

There are some virtues to this mindless mechanical interaction. One reason why human communication is so messy is that all the channels are operating simultaneously. The volume of information is so great that both speaker and listener filter what they receive through their expectations. If George was just fired and we expect him to be depressed, we may not notice that he's actually delighted—particularly if we ourselves are depressed for some reason. Psychological projection is a major factor in all human communications, and it causes all kinds of trouble. If we stop to think about it, erroneous communication is the rule rather than the exception. Whole groups of people may pursue a course of action that no person likes, because each assumes the others are in favor of it. Our assumptions constantly get us into trouble.

And, finally, when mindless mechanical work is appropriate, it's difficult to obtain. A typist will add new typing errors, as well as fix old ones. A draftsman may insert mistakes not previously there.

So we shouldn't be too quick to denigrate the literal-mindedness of the computer. It has value in some situations—precisely because it is so different from human interaction.

Mistakes

As a rule, computers don't make mistakes. People make mistakes.

Some argue that an incorrect forecast from a computer weather-forecasting system is an example of a computer mistake. Such a view ignores the fact that a person wrote the program to carry out the weather forecast; the machine merely did the dirty work.

At least for now, the old adage still holds: it's a poor workman who blames his tools. And a computer is just a tool.*

Monitor

Unless your computer has a switched plug at the back, don't buy a monitor that lacks an on/off light. You'll forget and leave it on for days at a time. Also, be wary of buying a color monitor to display text. Color monitors are generally unsatisfactory for text displays. If you want to view both color graphics and text, you probably need two monitors.

Of the monochromatic monitors, there is heated and pointless debate about whether white, green, or amber lettering is easiest on the eye. It's a question of personal preference: look at them and decide for yourself.

---

*There is, however, one technical area where computers can indeed make a mistake. Oddly enough, it's fundamental—in arithmetic. If you divide 1 by 3, the answer is .3333333333 . . . with the 3's continued indefinitely. Computers, like people, must round off. But how they round off, and how they handle decimal points in general, varies slightly from one machine to another. You're not likely to have a problem from this, but you might.

Need

"Do I need a computer?"

Probably not, unless you're in business. But you don't need a TV either, and you almost certainly have one. You don't need all the clothes you have. You own all sorts of things not strictly necessary for survival.

Need is totally subjective. It's a false issue.

The real question is "Am I going to be able to get through the rest of my life without a practical ability to use computers?" The answer is almost certainly "No."

Network

Interest in personal computers has usually focused on the individual's use of a so-called stand-alone machine. But within a few years, this may be less important than the fact that users around the country can be linked together over telephone lines in a network.

What's the advantage over simply making a call? Voice transmission is excellent for conveying emotional states, or limited amounts of hard data. But if you have ever listened as someone described a graphic image over the phone, you quickly realized that a picture is worth much more than a thousand words. And if anyone has tried to engage you in a complex discussion involving a lot of text or a great many figures, you probably found yourself postponing the conversation until you had a copy of the information in front of you. Furthermore, telephone calls must be arranged at a time suited to both parties. And you cannot just "put information out there"; you must call a particular person.

Computer networks have none of these disadvantages. You

can transmit text or graphics at your convenience; the receiver can review the information at his. You can put information out onto a network "bulletin board" and whoever is interested (including people you don't know) can pick it up and use it, and communicate back to you.

Computer conferencing and specialized user groups of all sorts are springing up. Small computers may ultimately be as ubiquitous as telephones, because they are as useful as telephones—for communicating with other people.

Notebook

Keep a notebook for your machine. Whenever you get stuck and have to look something up, or whenever you discover a neat trick or come upon some funny little time-saver, write it down. All machines and all programs have their little quirks. But you'll forget, and in six months you'll encounter the same problem, and have to go through the whole searching process all over—except that this time you'll remember you once knew the answer. If only you'd written it down . . .

Operating System

The concept of an operating system confuses many users. Fine, there's a computer waiting to be told what to do. Fine, you load a program into the computer and the program tells the computer what to do. Then where does this operating system fit in?

Next you learn that certain programs require a particular operating system, not a particular machine. Some operating systems, such as CP/M, are referred to as "popular," as if the operating system were a thing to be embraced in its own right. If your machine doesn't "run under" a particular operating system, you may be able to buy something that will see that it does. But what *is* the operating system?

It's easiest to think of operating systems as a form of government. All governments govern, but a constitutional monarchy, a democracy, and a dictatorship differ in the details of how the job is done.

The operating system governs the internal workings of the computer, which is why operating systems are sometimes called an "environment," and why computers "run under" an operating system the way nations run under a dictatorship. By changing the operating system, you change the internal workings of the computer—in particular, you change the way the computer reads in and writes back to floppy disks.

The operating system is pretty much invisible to the user. You treat the computer the same way no matter what you're running under. The significance of the operating system lies in the programs that can run on your machine.

The most widely accepted operating system is CP/M, which stands for Control Program/Microprocessors. CP/M was created by Digital Research, and an enormous range of programs has been created that run under it. If your machine can run under CP/M, then you have access to all these programs; if not, you don't, and never will. Thus, the availability of CP/M—whether you need it right now or not—is a significant feature to consider when buying a computer.

Unix, another operating system, was created by Bell Labs in the 1960s and is gaining popularity. The principal advantage of Unix is that it is extremely portable—programs developed on one machine are easily converted to another. Its immediate usefulness, however, is not as clear as that of CP/M.

Maybe you'll never need the programs that run under a particular operating system like CP/M. But you can't be sure—and the experience of previous computer users is that they end up using their machines for purposes they never imagined when they first bought the machines.

Outmoded

Nothing prevents people from getting involved with computers more than the fear that whatever they learn or buy will soon be obsolete. Such concerns are heightened by reports emphasizing the rapidity with which machines and programs are changing. Advertisers promote the newness and the relentless pace of advance.

In fact, fear of obsolescence is a largely groundless concern. People imagine quantum jumps in machine development that simply don't occur. While it is true that machines become ever smaller, cheaper, and easier to use, they are not *that much* smaller, cheaper, or easier to use. It's more to the point to think about computers as you think about cars or refrigerators: subsequent models will always be better, but a sensible purchase will not look like a Model T by the time you get it home.

If you have a use for a computer now, then buy a machine that fills your needs and don't worry about the future. In three or five years, you may want a newer computer, but in the meantime you will have had the benefit of your present machine. This is especially so for small-business applications, where a computer will often pay for itself in the first year.

I can report two anecdotes from personal experience. In 1980, I was thinking about buying an Apple II computer. A friend who seemed to know a lot about computers told me, "Don't buy an Apple II, wait for the Apple III. It'll be out any day now." Like a good consumer, I dutifully waited more than a year for the Latest Thing. But when the Apple III finally appeared, it was clearly a business machine, not suited to my interests at all. I'd wanted an Apple II all along, and I'd wasted a year waiting for the wrong thing.

The second story is the reverse. In 1979, I bought an Olivetti word processor. This was at a time of rapid change in word-processing technology; IBM was about to come out with a word processor; my friends asked why I was not waiting for the Latest Thing. But I knew my needs; I was satisfied that the Olivetti would do what I wanted, and I bought it and was done with it.

I'm writing this book on that same word processor, now four years old. Newer word processors are much cheaper and somewhat smaller, and offer many features that my Olivetti lacks. But after four years, there has been no development sufficiently compelling to induce me to buy a new word processor. In another couple of years, there may be.

So be careful about obsolescence. If you're not sensible, you'll fall into the Housewife's Fallacy: don't clean the house, because it will only get dirty again anyway.

Paranoia

As you begin to feel comfortable with your machine, you will have to deal with the paranoia of others. Perhaps you'll talk about your machine at cocktail parties and dinners—computers do tend to be compelling. You'll see the eyes of non-computer people glaze over. You may get snide comments and hostile remarks, perhaps an idiotic opinion or two.

Be gentle. Remember you were that way six months ago. And try to imagine that six months from now, when you're a more seasoned veteran, you may have to listen to the blithering enthusiasm of some newcomer—one of those tedious people who think computers are the salvation of the world, and can't stop talking about them.

Parents

You've just bought a home computer, but before you've even figured out how to turn the damn thing on, your seven-year-old daughter starts banging away at it, making it do all kinds of tricks.

If you're a parent who has any tendency to feel competitive with your children, or to regard your children as evidence that you're aging and over the hill, such an experience can be hugely disturbing. It's easy to make more of it than you should.

Your son or daughter's ease with computers probably reflects a year or more of experience at school. After a year of experience, you'll be comfortable, too. But what to do in the meantime?

Getting your child to teach you is not as simple as it sounds. Many parents fear losing authority over their kids, and hesitate to adopt a subordinate role—ever. And kids make impatient teachers; after hearing "Oh, Dad, don't do *that*" a couple of times, you may decide to salvage what's left of your ego and study the manual on your own. Now you're sitting up at night in bed, tired from a day at the office and trying to make sense of a goddamn manual filled with hieroglyphics. The more you compare your struggles to the easy familiarity of your child, the more annoyed you become. Eventually you hate the computer, and your smart-ass know-it-all offspring as well.

Parents who successfully overcome this situation seem to do so in several ways:

1. *They take a class.* There are good reasons to go outside the family structure for certain kinds of education. It's often more comfortable to learn a new skill from someone who is not mixed up in the strong emotions of family life. An evening class from an adult instructor is much more straightforward. Your kid learned about computers from someone else. You might as well learn from someone else, too.

2. *They buy a different machine.* If your kids are using TRS-80s at school, buy an Apple or an Atari for your home. There are enough quirks and differences from one machine to another to slow your kid down, and to make it possible for you to learn with him.

3. *They make the child a consultant.* You start out with your machine, learning as best you can on your own. When you get stuck, you ask your child for specific help. But you don't expect the child to teach you everything from start to finish.

4. *They learn on weekends.* Astutely, you avoid the machine

on weekday evenings, when you are tired. It's then that you're likely to snap at a child who rattles off an explanation and makes you feel dumb. Learning a computer is difficult; you need to be rested. And children have homework on weeknights; they may resent parental interruptions and be less tolerant than on weekends.

In the end, parents who find a way to permit their children to help them have an enormous advantage. It's much easier to learn to use a computer with individual help. If your child can be a helper and not an antagonist, you'll learn much more quickly and easily.

In fact, if you check around the office, you'll be amazed at how many people are learning about computers from their kids. They've managed to work it out. So can you.

Portable

Most machines are less portable than they look—and most people don't need a portable machine.

Although the salesman assures you that businessmen everywhere lug their Apple computer and two disk drives to the office every morning and home to the kids every night, don't be so sure. It's heavy, and it's a pain in the neck to detach and hook up. A truly portable machine must be very compact and light—but then you may find yourself going blind staring at a miniature screen.

In any case, it's never been clear to me who really needs to pull out his computer and run programs in a car or on an airplane, except somebody desperate for novelty. In my view, the whole idea of a computer is that it enables you to get your work done so fast that you can sit back and enjoy the ride.*

---

*But if you really require a portable machine, wait as long as you can before buying. This year's eighteen-pound, briefcase-size machine will be next year's nine-pound, book-size machine. Extremely small, powerful computers are evolving very rapidly at this writing.

Power

"I have 40K of ROM!"
   "I have 256K of RAM!"
   "I have a 10-megabyte Winchester drive!"
   "I have a high-speed color printer!"
   "I have a 16-bit CPU!"
   "I have FORTH!"
There's only one response to this kind of bragging. Your big powerful machine is only as good as what you do with it—which is another matter entirely.

Power, Electrical

If you're like me, you've spent your whole life ignoring manufacturers' advice to ground your appliances; your wall sockets are a messy tangle of extension cords and three-way plugs.

But computers won't put up with that cavalier attitude. They are sensitive to the electricity they receive. They must be grounded, and they must have reasonably constant power without surges or dropouts. If you live in an old building or in a community with fluctuating electrical power, you may have to take steps to insure that your power is more stable. This can involve anything from buying a surge suppressor to hiring an electrician to run a dedicated electrical line to your wall socket.

It's also worth remembering that the majority of computer failures are really power failures—they occur because you've developed a loose connection somewhere. Before you drag your machine back to the store, make sure all your plugs and cable connections are seated snugly. If that doesn't fix it, unplug your machine, remove the cover, and press down firmly on all the little chips with your thumb. If you've got expansion boards or modules, press these down as well. Then put the cover back on, power up, and see if it works. Chances are it will.

Print

Old-fashioned print—books and newspapers—will be with us for some time to come.

There are several reasons to think so. First, printed text on paper is ideally suited for browsing. This is how most people use a newspaper; they don't really read it, they look through it. Browsing is far slower and more difficult when electronic text is displayed on a video screen.

Second, print is highly portable. You can read it on trains and planes and buses with no additional equipment or power source.

Finally, as a medium, print is cheap. The cost of a paperback book is less than a floppy disk containing the equivalent information.

Even computer people agree that we'll be reading print on paper for at least ten more years—which is an eternity in the computer world.

Printer

In descending order of cost, there are three kinds of printers—letter-quality printers, dot-matrix printers, and thermal printers.

Letter-quality or Daisy-wheel printers work like regular typewriters: a metal element presses a ribbon against the page to make the character. They are expensive, slow, and often unnecessary. A letter-quality printer costs at least a thousand dollars more than other printers.

Thermal printers burn letters with heat into special paper.

Thermal printers are silent. If that's essential, get one. Otherwise don't. Print quality is poor; the paper is expensive and turns dark with age.

Most people choose a dot-matrix printer. This printer presses a matrix of pinpoint dots against a ribbon, thus stamping the letter shape on the paper.

Dot-matrix printers come in a bewildering variety. Most print different type sizes; some print colors; and many print graphics. Most stores carry books of printout from different printers, to help you choose. Make sure you see the printer do all the things you want it to do before you buy it.

At the same time, you'll see how easy the printer is to use. Most are simple, but a few require tricky programming commands that are annoying and troublesome.

Buyers often ignore printing speed. This is because the printer in the store seems to be clattering away like blazes. And it is: the human speed-typing record is 186 words per minute, or roughly 17 characters per second. Even the slowest printer will go twice that fast, printing 35 or 45 characters per second.

But speed is the forte of computers, and as you work with your machine, you'll change your notions of how fast things should be done. Dot-matrix printers average 80–120 characters per second, and some will print 200 characters per second. Remember that nobody ever feels his printer is too fast.

Finally, printers differ widely in sturdiness: ask the salesman which models are tough. He has no reason to suggest an unreliable printer; unreliable printers come back—literally—to haunt him. Remember that a high-strung sports car may be your pride and joy, but a high-strung printer is just a pain.

"Problems with Our Computer"

It's happened to everyone. On your monthly statement, you find a charge for a book, dress, or piece of equipment that you never ordered, or long ago returned, or already paid for.

You call the company and somebody says, "We're having problems with our computer." He asks for your forgiveness, and a copy of your canceled check or other documentation.

You do as requested, but the next month the item is still there —with an added interest charge. You call again, but the person you talked to before is at lunch, on vacation, or "no longer with us."

The new person says he is having problems with the computer, and asks for documentation. You say you already sent it; he says he can't find it. You send the documentation again.

But pretty soon you get a letter from Moe's Collection Agency that begins, "We're sure a nice person like you doesn't mean to be a creepy deadbeat . . ."

You call again. Everyone you've ever talked to is out to lunch or on vacation or "no longer with us." The new person on the phone checks your account and says, "Well, you *are* awfully late in paying. . . ." When you explain the whole story, the person is very sympathetic and says they are having problems with the computer, and please send the documentation all over again.

This can go on for years.

Of course, there are times when a company really has computer problems, but you can recognize those times immediately. The person on the phone or behind the desk is scared and exhausted—he's been taking complaints like yours for hours. He's scared because he knows they really *do* have a problem, a massive one. He's probably hoping you won't figure out just how bad it is. He'll beg for mercy. Be merciful.*

But if the person is glib in citing "problems with our computer," then you're just getting the runaround. Remember that computers don't make mistakes; people do. The computer didn't lose your earlier letters and copies of canceled checks; the computer didn't fail to remove the erroneous entry. You're not dealing

---

*And be honest. If you read between the lines and figure out that all the March billings are shot to hell, you'll realize that you could refuse to pay not only one disputed entry but the entire month's billings. Don't take advantage of his vulnerability. Remember, this month it's his company that has the computer problem. Next month, it could be yours.

with a computer problem at all—you're dealing with a sloppy, inept company. And you're allowing their ineptitude to waste your time and energy.

Don't do it.

When you receive a wrong billing, give the company the benefit of the doubt. This means you make *one* phone call, and send *one* letter if requested. Send the letter to the person you talked to, and begin with "Following our phone conversation today . . ." Keep the originals of everything—your correspondence, your bills, your canceled checks. Send them Xeroxes.

If the problem isn't fixed within one month, don't get mad—but don't waste any more time with these turkeys either. Send a second copy of all your correspondence and bills directly to the president of the company. Include a pleasant, straightforward letter indicating that you have taken appropriate steps to correct the error, but since this has not worked, you're asking his office to clear up a problem within his company.

Don't apologize for wasting his time; and don't hesitate to write, even if it's a five-dollar discrepancy. In my experience, such letters to the president invariably solve the "problem with our computer."

It's amazing how many company presidents know how to fix computers.

Processing, Data

No matter how much money you invested in your super-duper computer, no matter how bright the genius who wrote your program, data processing is only as good as the data being processed.

The computer expression GIGO means "Garbage In, Garbage Out." This great truth has become a great cliché. The people who think they understand it are the ones who most often get into trouble.

Obviously, if an operator enters the wrong figures into a program, he'll get wrong answers back. Everybody knows that. The problems arise when figures entered aren't exactly wrong—they're just imprecise, and everyone knows it. For example, if you estimate next year's business, you may enter a series of guesses, each within 10 percent. These entries aren't garbage; as far as you're concerned, they're pretty good guesses. The natural tendency is to assume that the final projection is accurate to the same degree. But it may not be.

If you add your estimates, the potential error remains the same. Ten entries, each accurate within 10 percent, produce a final answer that is accurate within 10 percent. But if your estimates are multiplied with each other, the possible error increases rapidly. Ten entries, each estimated within 10 percent and multiplied together, may give a final error as large as 300 percent. Thus, your final estimate isn't very reliable, even if it came out of a computer.

It may be worthwhile to go through the estimating process for other reasons. But it is a clear mistake to believe the final computer projection. Why do people sometimes believe it? Because almost nobody wants to admit that his business life is so unpredictable, so uncertain. But it is. That's the truth—not your computer projection.

Processing, Word

Word-processing technology has been around for more than ten years, but it's only now becoming popular. A word processor looks like a typewriter with a TV screen. As you type, words appear on the screen, instead of on the page. Because the words are retained in the computer memory as electrical impulses, they can be manipulated with great flexibility. You can add, delete, or modify text at the press of a button. You can create blocks of text and combine them however you want—to make form letters or legal documents. As you make changes, the computer continuously realigns your text, re-forms paragraphs, and adjusts your page count.

There are a few odd tricks, such as "search and destroy." You can instruct the word processor to search your entire text for a word, to find every instance and make changes. (I didn't want "software" to proliferate in this book, and I used my word processor to check that it didn't appear except in specific instances. Meanwhile I went off and had a cup of coffee.) Word processors can also check spelling and identify typos.

The two questions people ask most often about word processors are: how long does it take to learn to use one, and will it make a difference to my writing?

If you already know how to type, it'll take two to five days to learn to use a word processor—roughly the time it would take you to become comfortable with a slightly different typewriter keyboard, so that your finger hits the backspace key instead of the return key, and so on. This makes sense, because a word processor is really just a fancy typewriter that performs secretarial functions. People who say it takes weeks to learn are exaggerating to impress you with their newly acquired skill. If you install a machine on Monday, you'll be whizzing along by Wednesday or Thursday. Actually, the most troublesome thing for beginners to learn is not to hit the carriage return at the end of a line, since the machine does that automatically.

Does it make a difference in your writing? It's markedly faster, especially for revisions. Copy is clean. But whether the computer makes a more profound difference depends on whom you talk to —and when. For the first six months or so, the wonders of the new machine are so impressive to the user that he may claim virtues that don't really exist. As time passes and the machine becomes more familiar, the process of writing starts to seem the same after all.

There's not much difference between the blank page and the blank screen.

Program

A set of instructions to make the computer do something. But that's not a very useful way to think of a program, since instructions purely to the machine for its own use are often brief.

The bulk of many programs is devoted to helping people put data into the machine and get processed information back out again. One's satisfaction with a program strongly reflects these areas of input and output.

People don't understand this. When they look at a long program, they fail to recognize how much of it is directly geared to them. Don't throw up your hands: this stuff matters to you. And it's always the least computery part of the program.

For example, a BASIC program might begin with:

```
10   HOME
20   VTAB 3: HTAB 5
30   PRINT "WHAT IS YOUR NAME?"; : INPUT N$
40   PRINT N$
50   PRINT "IS YOUR NAME CORRECT? (Y/N)"; : INPUT A$
60   IF A$ = "N" THEN GOTO 20
70   PRINT "NICE TALKING WITH YOU,"; N$ ; "."
```

Now, this means in English:

10   Clear the screen

20   Tab down 3 lines, and horizontally five spaces.

30   Print "What is your name?" and stay on the same line. Wait for something to be typed in from the keyboard. Call whatever is input N$.

40   Print this N$ back out again, whatever it is.

50   Print "Is your name correct? (Y/N)." This prompts the user to answer Y or N. Get the answer, and call it A$.

60   If the answer is N for no, then you'll need to start all over again. So go back to line 20.

70   If the answer is not N, then the name must be okay. So print "Nice talking with you," and stay on the same line. Print the name N$, stay on the same line, and print a period (.).

Notice that the BASIC program is not mathematical. It's much like instructing a typist. VTAB means vertical tab, HTAB means horizontal tab. PRINT means print what's in quotes. INPUT means wait for input. And so on. You don't need differential calculus to follow this.

And in any case, the whole routine is for your (the user's) benefit, to allow you to enter and check your input. Therefore you may want to modify it. You can do all this without paying any attention to the guts of the program that appear later on.

There's a corollary to this. If you're commissioning programmers to write programs for you, you may be frustrated at the delay between the time the programmer announces the program is "working" and the time it actually accepts data and spits back answers.

The reason is that the programmer is focused, at least in part, on the internal workings of the machine and how it manipulates data. This aspect is invisible to you. You're focused on what you put in and what you get back. Programmers always consider the program to be working before the input and output routines are finished. Because these input/output routines are extensive, it may take a long time to get them right.

Programmers, Supervising of

Programming has become a feared and hated art. There are endless disaster stories, all unnecessary. If you hire programmers to write a program for you, here are some rules to follow:

1. Hire one person. If additional people are required, let that person hire them and supervise their work.

2. Hire a programmer who speaks ordinary English. If he insists on talking about bytes and algorithms, don't employ him.

The days of the Priesthood of the Machine are long gone. Get someone you can talk to.

3. Hire a programmer who doesn't know your business. If a programmer has previously written programs for businesses similar to yours, you might think it advantageous to hire him. It's more likely a liability. There is nothing worse than a programmer who assumes he understands what you are about, and what your needs are. The essence of good programming is a fresh look at the situation.

4. Hire a programmer who is familiar with your equipment, or the language that your other programs are written in. Familiarity with your business is a drawback; but familiarity with your computer is a definite advantage.

5. Be prepared to spend time working with the programmer. If you want a system that fits your needs, you are going to have to take the time to identify your needs. A good programmer will be skilled at getting this out of you.

The core of your discussions should be: "What do you do and why do you do it?" Other questions to be considered are: "What parts of your job do you like and what parts don't you like? What always seems to get done late or badly? What always goes smoothly? What do you never want to do again? What's your fantasy of how your job could be done?" Anecdotes and examples should be encouraged.

Productive sessions with the programmers are invariably painful. Because you must explain your most fundamental (and generally unquestioned) assumptions, and your most trivial and automatic routines, you will find these talks exhausting and difficult. If they are not exhausting and difficult, you're not going deeply enough. I suspect the advantage of putting a business on a machine derives as much from re-examination of old methods as it does from the actual transfer of work to a computer. Frequent sessions lasting one to two hours are best.

6. Feel free to modify your ideas as you go along. Changing your mind about what you want the computer to do is inevitable. This is no time to be an unswerving leader. Swerve all you want.

7. Resist altering your work patterns merely to make it easier for the machine. Every programmer will sooner or later see a simplifying maneuver that makes his own life easier, and he will promote it vigorously. But the whole point is to have the machine conform to you, not vice versa.

On the other hand, if a genuinely improved way of doing things emerges, adopt it.

8. Break down the programmer's work into sub-units and set deadlines for completion of each unit. Review progress in detail at least once a month; every two weeks is better. Anyone who turns a programmer loose for six months without supervision is asking for problems.*

9. Expect it to take longer than you expect. Some people say a programmer can write only ten lines of finished, debugged code per day. Anyhow, it's a slow undertaking. It always takes longer than they tell you it will, and longer than you think it should.

10. Insist that your program be well documented at every stage of development. Don't wait until it's done, because you may have to fire the programmer before completion. At least half the disaster stories of custom programming involve poorly documented programs that prove unmodifiable later because no one can figure them out.

11. Recognize that programmers are strange folk. They work at home, or at night, or for sustained periods followed by sustained absences. A nine-to-five programmer is a contradiction in terms.

12. Finally, if such things matter, agree in advance about who

---

*At these review meetings, insist he go through a hard copy of the source code with you and explain to you in general terms how the program is set up. Even if you don't really understand the code (and you won't), this procedure has at least five benefits.

First, the programmer will respond positively to your interest; he'll end up working better and faster. Second, as he explains his work aloud, he often notices problems he hasn't considered—without your saying a word. Third, programmers tend to drift, refining minor parts of the program while neglecting the guts. You'll keep him on track with frequent review. Fourth, you'll see if he's documenting sufficiently, and if new work is being done. Fifth, you'll learn from the interaction.

Even though you may lack specialized computer knowledge, it's still your job to supervise the programmer. He needs supervision—and support and encouragement—as much as anyone else. Give it to him.

owns the program, and who has the rights to use or market it. Just because you have paid someone to write a program does not necessarily mean you own it.

Recovery

Recovery refers to techniques to get back lost data on a floppy disk. There are three things to know about data recovery.

The first is that it's possible. If the data was ever recorded on the disk, the fact that you've mistakenly erased a file, found your dog chewing the disk, or suffered some other screwup does not mean the data is lost forever. There is a whole range of programs and tricks to help you get it back. Copy the injured disk if you can, and then go through the recovery maneuvers. If you don't succeed, get help from a computer store, or from the manufacturer of the machine or program. It's actually rather rare for lost data to be truly unrecoverable.

The second thing is that data recovery is always a last resort. It's inherently unreliable; even if it works, the data is likely to come back scrambled. And even simple recovery takes a huge amount of time.

The third thing is that if you have a backup disk, then you haven't got a problem. Just copy the backup onto the original and carry on. If you don't have a backup, you've asked for the trouble you now have.*

---

*But if you elect to recover the disk—and if you succeed—never copy the recovered disk onto your original backup. Instead, make a new backup. The reason is that a recovered disk may contain hidden glitches or deletions that only become evident days or weeks later. When you hit these problems, you'll wish you'd kept the original backup.

Retrofit

Certain terms are chosen to disguise their real meaning. "Retrofit" is engineering jargon that sounds high-tech and scientific. But in computer terms, it usually means correcting what wasn't done right in the first place.

"Enhancement" is a similar word. Additions to a computer system can modify or improve it, but when something is added to make the machine competitive with other computers in its class, that's called an enhancement.

Whenever enhancements are retrofitted at no charge, or very slight charge, you can be pretty sure what's really going on.

Scientific Models

Human beings continually create models of reality. These models are always simplified and approximate, although we tend to forget that. Models are integral to our language and our tools. If we say a friend is angry, we ignore the fact that our friend is much more than just the emotion of anger. If we measure with a yardstick, we ignore the fact that the yardstick is inexact.

Because we use models constantly, and because models are built into our language, we tend to substitute models—simplified constructs of reality—for reality itself. In minor ways, we've all had the experience of seeing our models collapse, as when the furniture doesn't fit in a room because our measurements were inexact, or when our angry friend tells a joke to his supposed enemy. At those times, we are sharply reminded that reality is more complex than our modeled version of it.

Computers enable us to create models of previously unimagined intricacy. Such models can be enormously seductive; they don't collapse before our eyes in any obvious way. A classic example is Joseph Weizenbaum's program ELIZA, which instructs a computer to simulate a therapist. The program fooled a great many people into thinking that a new era of automated therapy was about to begin. Many otherwise sensible scientists advocated just that.

It is in precisely such postures that scientific bias becomes dangerous. Science is an enormously powerful method for exploring reality, but it is only one method. Whole realms of human experience lie beyond its grasp. In fact, consciousness itself is beyond science, as George Wald recently observed.

The failure to recognize this leads to patent absurdities. A team of scientists measuring the heartbeat and rectal temperature of a yogi in a trance state is a profound joke. Yet the scientists are doing the best they can; in fact, they are doing the only things they can. They are in the same position as social scientists who study garbage to determine how people lead their lives; such studies tell you something, but not much. The scientific approach misses the point.

It often does—more often, perhaps, than we are willing to admit. We have a strong tendency to exclude or deny phenomena that don't fit our pre-existing schemes.

When I studied surgery at a Boston teaching hospital, two well-known surgeons were much discussed by the students.

Surgeon A was a brilliant academician who operated with classic perfection. He worked quickly, performing an operation in the standard time, or faster. He worked neatly, not disturbing the tissue any more than necessary, tying off vessels with a minimum of excess tissue left over. He kept anaesthesia light, and rigorously observed sterile procedure.

Surgeon B was a former football star with the easygoing casualness of the ex-jock. He broke every rule. He poked around inside the patient, taking twice as long as other surgeons to perform an operation. His messy surgical ties left behind lots of excess tissue. He kept his patients deeply drugged with anaesthesia, and he occasionally coughed into the field.

But Surgeon B's patients were invariably up and around immediately after the operation, happy and smiling and on their way home in record time. And Surgeon A's patients had terrible postoperative problems: they got infections, they got complications, they whined and complained, their hospital stays dragged on for weeks.

This disparity between technique and results was well known throughout the hospital. No one argued the facts. The question was why did it happen? We students were taught that surgical speed, minimal trauma, light anaesthesia, and scrupulous cleanliness were the keys to good operative results.

Yet here was evidence that it wasn't so. Nor could it be explained away by differences in bedside manner. Surgeon A was attentive and reassuring to his patients; Surgeon B spent little time with them, and frequently didn't bother to visit them the night before a procedure. This behavior didn't affect the outcome—nor did it matter to the patients themselves. Ordinarily, patients would scream neglect until the surgeon came; Surgeon B's patients would just shrug and say he was probably busy and they'd see him in the morning.

What was happening? How did it work, and how could you explain it? If it wasn't the science of medicine and it wasn't the art of medicine, what was it?

Nobody ever figured it out. The best we could conclude was that Surgeon B, in some mysterious way, instilled in his patients the *expectation* that everything would be fine and the surgery would go well. But how he did this all-important thing, or when, was unknown.

Unable to provide an explanation, we settled for a description and pretended that it was an explanation as well. But the suspicion remained that what we were observing lay somehow outside science and its methods. Such notions were uncomfortable and we did not dwell on them. Powerless to understand the situation better, we resumed the study of what we could do: learning to make good ties, work quickly, use light anaesthesia, follow sterile procedure, and so on.

I don't regard this situation as unique in any way. But if you have only two categories for what you perceive in the world—

science or superstition—then you are obliged to conclude either that the differences in results between Surgeon A and Surgeon B did not really exist, or that some crucial difference in technique did exist but we hadn't found it.

In the meantime, practicing surgeons all recognize that some of their colleagues have the touch, and others don't. The healing touch. Whatever that means.

Will a computer help you find it? Perhaps it won't. The computer is a product of science, and it's most easily used to create models that fit the scientific world view. There's nothing wrong with that —so long as the power of the machines does not seduce us into allowing the machines to define reality for us.

Bertrand Russell once argued that reality is not mathematical, it's just that we're too stupid to understand anything but those parts of reality that can be explained in mathematical terms. In the same way, the computer is a powerful tool for exploring aspects of reality—but not every aspect of reality. Personally, I find it interesting to divert a computer to frankly non-rational tasks; a program to cast the I Ching is included in the appendices. You can play with it and decide for yourself if a three-thousand-year-old unscientific Chinese tradition is superstition or not.

There are many ways of looking at reality. Science is only one way. The most profound experiences of human life lie beyond science—and beyond computers. This does not diminish either science or computers.

It's just a perspective.

Skills, Computer

At the moment, only one skill is essential to operate a computer: the ability to type. This will probably remain so for ten years.

This situation affects women more than men, since women have been raised to think of typing as a low-grade, secretarial skill.

It was probably good advice when Mother or some well-wishing male executive told you never to learn to type. But now that typing is the primary skill for computer interaction, it suddenly has no social connotations whatever. Secretaries type, presidents type, chairpersons of the board type.

If you can't type, you're at a disadvantage.

Learn to type.

Social Change

At this stage in the twentieth century, we can be excused a certain amount of cynicism—and a certain amount of fear—about the impact of still another new technology, computers, on our lives.

Certainly computers are here to stay; certainly more and more of us will be looking at screens as we work. But what will result from this is unclear. There seem to be competing views for every aspect of this development. For example:

More people will work at home, so home life will become more important. That seems good. But keeping everyone at home will make it difficult to get any time alone. That seems bad. But women raising children can work at home conveniently. That seems good. But they'll be staring at the screens, not the kids. That seems bad.

In education computers are compelling, so kids learn quickly on them. That seems good. But the computers are so compelling they're addicting. That seems bad.

Computers can handle a lot of data quickly. That seems good. But that fluid data is vulnerable to theft or destruction. That seems bad. A computerized society will be swift and efficient. That seems good. But we will be dependent on the machines. That seems bad.

Computers are becoming more humanlike in their responses. That seems good. But as they become more humanlike in their responses, they may become just as much of a pain in the neck as people. That seems bad.

Computers will put people out of work. That seems bad.

But computers will assist in the retraining process. That seems good.

And so it goes.

What is one to make of these conflicting views? My own feeling is that all views are right. The computer revolution is affecting every aspect of society and it will produce a mixture of good and bad effects.

Such a conclusion may seem like cheating. It certainly feels unsatisfactory. We'd all prefer a clean simple line into the future, straight as time's arrow. The fact that the clean lines drawn by past generations proved wrong does not seem to diminish our own desire for clean lines. But history suggests that how we shape our lives to a new technology is complex, and ultimately unpredictable. It is easier to anticipate the arrival of a new technology than it is to predict what will happen to the societies that use it.

Or, put another way, what happens is in our hands—individually. Yours and mine and our neighbors'.

Software

I avoid this 1950s slang term, which should have been buried with Eisenhower.

In the old days, machines were "hardware," and the programs to run on the machines, generally punch cards or tapes, were cutely termed "software." There was a clear physical difference between hardware and software.

But over the years the distinction has become confused, especially with the advent of the Programmable Read-Only Memory (PROM) chip, whereby what is clearly software is converted into what is demonstrably hardware. Some programs are now sold as chips, which you plug into your machine. The term "firmware" has been introduced to refer to this hard software.

I prefer to talk about machines and programs, and forget

what's hard and what's soft. "Software" always conjured up images of rubber table settings for me, anyway.*

Specialized Knowledge and the Professions

Why do we consult a doctor or a lawyer? In part, at least, because the professional person possesses specialized knowledge we need. This specialized knowledge is generally highly formal in its structure.

Because computers can easily store and manipulate formal information, professional knowledge is extremely vulnerable to computers. That should have been obvious as soon as pocket language translators appeared five years ago. If you can encode the formal rules for language translation on a microchip, you can encode the formal rules for divorce proceedings or appendicitis diagnosis on a microchip as well. Once such a chip exists, it can be manufactured cheaply in quantity. Why should anyone consult a lawyer when he can buy all the information the lawyer possesses on a legal-knowledge chip for a couple of dollars?

Furthermore, in many situations the professional does not have all the expertise he needs. As more and more so-called expert systems help with legal research and medical diagnosis, the professional himself will be consulting the computer with increasing frequency. Since your doctor or lawyer is consulting a computer, why shouldn't you do it yourself, and skip the expensive middleman?

This question goes far beyond the age-old dream of getting rid

*There are two other reasons to discard the term "software." Software seems to imply something less important than hardware, when in fact software is usually more difficult, time-consuming, and expensive to create—hence the industry expression "It's the software that's hard." In addition, software programs are generally not soft and pliable at all. They're usually as rigid and unadaptable as if they were cast in iron.

of doctors and lawyers. In the end, it comes down to how we think about computers and people.

There's little question that in certain applications of specialized knowledge the computer can function as well as or better than its human counterpart. It's also true that the overwhelming majority of professional consultations are quite routine. The writing of wills, or the differential diagnosis of fatigue, is not complex.

But consider again our original question: why do we consult a doctor or a lawyer? In the most general sense, it is because something has gone wrong in our lives. Some personal relationship, or some aspect of our physical body, is not functioning correctly. We are uneasy and troubled, and we ask the professional to restore function and balance to our lives. Although we may imagine that this consultation is a characteristic of complex societies, it can be found in the simplest societies as well.

The Huni Kui people of the Amazon* are a tribe of jungle hunters. From time to time, a member of the tribe becomes unable to catch game for his family. Either the hunter finds no animals in his wandering, or the animals flee before he can shoot them, or his arrows miss their mark. If this continues long enough, the hunter's family suffers hardship and must be fed by others. The hunter himself is humiliated and indebted, until finally he is forced to consult the tribal chief.

This initiates a ritual interaction. The chief gathers the best hunters of the tribe. Together they examine the hunter's weapons, making sure that they are properly constructed and cared for. Then they inquire after the hunter's routine preparations for the hunt, what herbal baths and charms he employs. Next they review in minute detail his recent hunting failures. Finally, they all go into the jungle for an overnight ritual purification of the hunter and his weapons.

This ritual always works. The hunter invariably feels better and finds game. Order and balance are restored to the individual and the community.

---

*See F. Bruce Lamb, *The Wizard of the Upper Amazon* (Boston: Houghton Mifflin Co., 1975), p. 33.

Psychotherapy for a jungle hunter may seem a bizarre notion, but on closer examination we should be more surprised if it didn't occur. Every society requires mechanisms for integration of the members of that society.

But the point is that even in this technologically simple setting, the troubled person was obliged to go outside himself to experts for help. That help ultimately consisted of reintegrating the man with himself, his community, and his natural environment. This is a deeply human experience.

And when we consult doctors or lawyers, we seek the same kind of relief. Rarely is the goal merely access to information. We want advice, we want understanding, we want "someone we can talk to." It's common to feel better as soon as we've seen the doctor, even before we start taking the prescribed medication. And the lawyer who says "I'll handle it" makes us feel better, even before he actually takes any steps to solve the problem.

When professionals are viewed in this way, the importance of computers to professional interactions diminishes. We consult professionals not because we want information but because we want to feel better.

Can a computer make us feel better? Perhaps it can—if we allow ourselves some fundamental errors in perception.

In 1966, Joseph Weizenbaum, a computer scientist at MIT, wrote ELIZA, one of the most famous and significant programs in computer history. ELIZA instructs a computer to imitate a non-directional, Rogerian therapist. In the years since, many versions of ELIZA have been written for small computers. Here is a recent interaction on mine:

HELLO THERE, I'M ELIZA. HOW ARE YOU FEEL-ING?

I'm tired today.

WHY ARE YOU TIRED TODAY?

From working on my book.

HMMM . . . TELL ME MORE.

The book's about computers.

YOU THINK COMPUTERS CAUSE PROBLEMS FOR YOU?

Trying to explain that computers are stupid machines.

ARE YOU REFERRING TO ME?

Yes. You.

LET'S GET BACK TO YOUR PROBLEM . . .

Okay. Fine. Tell me my problem.

THERE ARE NO EASY ANSWERS TO YOUR PROBLEM.

You always say things like that.

HOW DOES THAT MAKE YOU FEEL?

I feel you don't care.

INTERESTING . . . CAN YOU ELABORATE ON SUCH FEEL-INGS?

Computers are just machines.

OH I THINK YOU KNOW BETTER THAN THAT.

Well, you aren't a human being, kiddo.

WHAT MAKES YOU THINK I AMENT A HUMAN BEING KIDDO

I rest my case.

DO YOU FEEL IT SOLVES ANYTHING TO REST YOUR CASE?

Although the responses sometimes appear complex, the computer is actually doing something rather simple. It scans the input sentence for key words it has been programmed to recognize. When it finds one, it selects an answer from a group of previously programmed responses. If the computer fails to find any word it knows, it gives a nondescript response such as HMMM . . . TELL

ME MORE. The whole process is utterly mechanical—and in this case, obviously so.

But more refined versions of ELIZA can be startlingly persuasive. It's not difficult to assume that the computer really understands you. Weizenbaum himself was alarmed by the initial acceptance of his program. Some users asked him to leave the room, because their conversation was becoming too intimate. Others refused to believe it was "just a program." Still others heralded ELIZA as initiating a new era of automated therapy.

This raises the question of what people think a therapist is. In *The Road Less Traveled,* psychiatrist M. Scott Peck* defines a therapeutic interaction that no machine could ever imitate, because that interaction is inherently, profoundly human. But unless we have conceived a view such as Peck's—unless we have developed a real sense of what a human being is, and what a caring human interaction is—then a chat with ELIZA will seem perfectly satisfactory.

In the future, we can expect a radical transformation in the professions, in which the exclusivity of information is denied the professional person while his therapeutic role continues unchanged. This strikes me as good. In the final analysis, we are not lawsuits to be tried or diseases to be treated; we are people with human problems. As we begin to have our own access to the professional's fund of information, we will naturally gravitate for further advice toward those professionals who treat us as human beings, and not merely as problems, or sources of income.

---

*Peck, M. Scott. *The Road Less Traveled* (New York: Simon and Schuster, 1978).

Speech, Computers and

In 1969, when my novel *The Andromeda Strain* was published, the idea of voice-reminder systems struck readers as exotic and bizarre.

But within ten years, Sharp sold a miniature talking clock with its voice circuits embedded in microchips; and by 1982, my Datsun spoke in a seductive female voice, informing me that "lights are on" or "fuel is low." By that time, many home computers had attachments that allowed them to speak in some fashion. But few computers could understand speech input in any flexible way.

How long will it be before you can talk to your computer as you do to your next-door neighbor? Most experts think that development awaits the so-called fifth-generation computers, at least ten years away. Even if you play the odds and assume development will occur twice as fast as the experts think, the first truly speech-responsive computer will not be available before 1988.

Meantime, face reality; learn to type.

Status, Computers and

When small computers first began to proliferate, about six years ago, most educated people adopted the traditional snobbish attitude toward machines. "I can't work them," they would say with pride. "My secretary [or assistant or middle manager] knows how to run it. I don't have the faintest idea."

These postures are straight out of *Hard Times,* and are appropriate to the Industrial Revolution of a hundred years ago, when operating machines was beneath persons of quality. Long after computer terminals appeared on secretarial and middle-management desks, vice-presidents would not be caught dead with terminals in their offices.

About two years ago, a transitional phase began—the hidden computer for top management. Like a wet bar or a television set, the computer was tucked away from casual view. Terminals were made to pop out of coffee tables, or from behind sliding wood panels. When top executives were portrayed as using computers in advertisements, the executives were reclining, feet propped up indolently on desk or ottoman, keyboard across their knees. No fevered hunching over a glowing terminal for the real decision makers!

Inevitably, computers became a status symbol in their own right. It's no longer fashionable to admit you can't use them, and everyone must have one prominently displayed to prove that he's with it and up-to-date.

These amusing fashion trends shouldn't be taken too seriously. Status symbols are not tools; they're status symbols, and one can argue that high-level executives should spend their time with people, not computers. But the traditional problem for managers is isolation—lack of access to the day-to-day, working reality inside their own organizations. From this standpoint, an executive who can't operate a computer is vulnerable. He must rely on subordinates to tell him what's happening.

My own feeling is that a good executive ought to be able to make a surprise visit to his own data bank, the way he makes a surprise visit to a regional office. But he shouldn't spend too much time at either place.

Tape

Having heard that disk drives are like sophisticated tape recorders, you won't be surprised to hear that ordinary tape recorders can be used to store computer programs. Most home computers will accept either disk drives or tape recorders for program storage. A few, like the Timex Sinclair 1000, only accept tape recorders.

Tape recorders are much cheaper than disk drives—and much inferior. Their principal defect is speed: they are much slower and more cumbersome than disk drives. Since speed is a primary advantage of the computer, a slow storage unit reduces the usefulness of the total system.

Tape is acceptable for an inexpensive system. But for most computers it's like playing a Bang & Olufsen receiver through pocket radio speakers: it works, but it doesn't do the machine justice.

Testing

Programs, like scientific theories, can never be proved right—they can only be found wrong. The fact that a program works a thousand times does not guarantee that a bug won't show up the next time.

Experienced programmers say, "There's always one more bug."

Test a new program until you're cross-eyed with exhaustion. And regard every running of a satisfactory program as one further test. There's no way around this perpetual testing and caution.

It's the nature of the beast.

Trust

Beginners go through all sorts of permutations of trust in their machines. Initially, as they see their precious data disappear onto a featureless plastic disk, they tend to print everything out "just to be safe." Later, as they grow more comfortable, they print less and less—and ignore warnings to make backup disks. Sooner or later, the computer crashes and they discover the error of their ways.

When people deal with processed computer data, a similar progression occurs. The first reports are viewed with profound suspicion, and later reports are accepted with blind faith.

Treat your computer like any other machine—your car or your dishwasher or your watch.

It's reliable as hell until the day it isn't.

User

To computer hackers, byte-heads, and other fanatics, the term "user" is a pejorative. It implies somebody who just uses the computer with no knowledge of how it operates.

If you're a user and somebody tries to make you feel bad because you don't know hexadecimal code, relax: users are the wave of the future. A certain number of people are fascinated by the computer and want to know everything about it, just as a certain number of people want to get dirty and greasy tinkering with their automobile engines on weekends. There's no harm in it, but there's no virtue in it either.

It's fine to be a user—simply to use the computer as a tool. There is a whole world of life and sensation and feeling that has nothing at all to do with computers. In fact, computers are really a rather trivial part of the human experience.

Don't let anyone tell you otherwise.

Widows, Computer

The little machines are incredibly compelling, and one can work them long into the night. Marriages fall apart because of the machines.

Here she comes at midnight, saying, "Honey, do you know what time it is?" You haven't the faintest idea and couldn't care less; without taking your eyes from the screen, you mutter something conciliatory and she goes away. She's back in two hours, stamping her foot, insisting you come to bed.

She's a computer widow, and you have a problem.

Your problem is getting easier—or, at least, more socially acceptable—all the time, because more and more spouses are faced with it, and they can discuss it among themselves while you go off and play with the machines.

But the problem of the computer widow or widower remains. And it awakens all the vague concerns people have that we will all eventually be engaged in some masturbatory act involving ourselves and our machine reflections, oblivious to everything in life that is flesh and blood and human and juicy and alive.

Such a fuzzy fear ignores several hard facts. People don't spend hours locked in embrace with their microwave ovens or their vacuum cleaners. There must be something special about computers that makes them so compelling. And there is.

A computer always listens to you. It reacts immediately, catching every nuance of what you say. It always hears you freshly. Each time you make a statement, it behaves as if you had never made that statement before.

On the other hand, close friends and loved ones don't respond freshly to what you say. They think they know you; familiarity breeds inattention, if not contempt. It's not hard to feel that the computer is "more alive," more attentive, than one's flesh-and-blood companions.

Further, the computer never gets tired. After three hours, it's just as quick to respond, and apparently just as interested, as it was during the first five minutes. It's an indefatigable playmate—every child's dream.

Finally, the computer makes no demands of its own. It is there to do what you want it to do, and when you get tired of it, you just turn it off. No guilt, no recriminations, just flip the switch and it's gone. It's a sort of intellectual prostitute—and the appeal of prostitutes has never been obscure.

My own feeling is that widows had better recognize what they're up against. And I can't help feeling that the competition between human beings and machines—for the attention of other human beings—can only benefit human beings in the long run. Computers are information-processing, communicating devices. And if they set a new standard for information processing and communication by human beings among themselves—well, we've needed that for a long time.

Zenith: The Final Days of Man Before the Machines Take Over?

Many theorists predict the eventual creation of a super-intelligent machine, a computer vastly more powerful than human beings. The machine might be constructed with biochips, and thus would literally be another life form.

We have already seen that such a computer is not imminent. But even if we imagine it in the distant future, how should we think about it?

My own feeling is that when the super-intelligent machine comes, we'll survive. We have always defined as human what is unique to us, and we have weathered these storms before.

We have no record of how human laborers felt when Neolithic domesticated animals took over as beasts of burden seven thousand years ago, but it's clear that mankind survived with dignity and a sense of humanness intact.

We have had machines for nearly two hundred years that did intricate tasks such as plucking, spinning, weaving. We seem to have survived that.

We've had computational machines for forty years, and we've survived that as well. That we now have robots to carry out still more complex tasks should not unduly distress us. Nor should the future prospect of a super-intelligent computer, a brain more powerful than ours.

We've been traveling down this road for a long time—perhaps as long as two million years. Making tools to free us to do something else with our hands, and our time.

A Zen meditation asks the question "What am I?" The meditator begins by saying, "I am not my hands, I am not my feet," then progresses through "I am not my body" and "I am not my thoughts" and "I am not my emotions." But as the meditation continues, breaking one kind of identification after another, there remains an "I" to deny what that "I" is. No matter how one continues this progression, no matter how far one extends it, there is always something left.

The fear that in the coming years we will be replaced entirely by our creations—that we will live with computers as our pets live with us—suggests an extraordinary lack of faith in human beings and their enterprise.

As far as we know, the universe is infinite.

As far as we know, we are the only creatures that know it's infinite.

As far as we know, our ancestors have worked patiently for hundreds of thousands, perhaps millions, of years to get us exactly where we are today.

As far as we know, we will always be greater than our creations. Our ancestors were threatened by trains and planes and electricity; we take these things for granted. Today we are threatened by computers; our descendants will take them for granted, too.

As far as we know, there is much about ourselves that we don't know.

Human beings will always have something else to do.

And so, for that matter, will their machines.

APPENDICES

APPLE APPENDIX

Taking Charge of an Apple II

The following routine can be done in two hours. You will need an Apple II, a disk drive, a System Master disk, and a blank disk.

You'll be entering programs, but I won't usually explain them. Don't let this worry you. Just type them in. The whole point is to show you what you don't need to understand.

Let's get started.

1. Turn the video monitor on. Without putting a disk in the drive, turn the computer on. (The switch is at the back of the machine.)

The screen will glow; the empty disk drive clatters. Find the RESET key and press it. Now you see a left bracket and a blinking square.* The bracket is the prompt; it means the machine is awaiting your instructions. So let's give it some instructions and show it who's boss.

2. At the keyboard, type PRINT 5 + 5. You will see this appear on the screen as you type. If you make a mistake in typing, just move the cursor back, using the arrow key, and retype it correctly.

You'll eventually have PRINT 5 + 5 on the screen, but nothing further happens. So press RETURN, the key that means "enter this instruction into the computer."

Instantly, you see "10" on the next line. This is encouraging—the stupid machine got it right.

3. Now type PRINT 5 * 5, and press RETURN. (The * means

---

*If you don't get the bracket and blinking square, hold down the CTRL key while pressing the RESET key, and then release both keys.

"multiply.") You receive a gratifyingly quick answer of "25." Try PRINT 5 — 5, and then PRINT 5 / 5. (The / means to "divide by.") Notice the machine consistently obeys you. But perhaps you feel it's too quick—maybe we should slow it down a little.

4. Type PRINT 5.01 * 5.02 — 5.03 / 2.04 * 100.05 + 3.06 + 20.07 — 200.08 + 300.09 / 1.10. Make sure you're hitting the zero key and not the letter "O." (On the screen, the zero key has a slash through it.) Press RETURN.

The answer comes back —125.682621—but not *quite* so instantaneously.

So far, we've simply proved that the computer can perform like a calculator. That's no big deal. What'll it do that a calculator can't?

5. Type PRINT "MICHAEL CRICHTON," and press RETURN. The machine prints my name. Make it print yours.

6. Now type:

```
FOR X = 1 TO 20 : HTAB X : PRINT "YOUR NAME
HERE" : NEXT
```

Fill in your name between the quotation marks. When you're sure the line is typed exactly right, press RETURN.

Not bad—although not exactly earth-shattering either. Anyway, the machine seems to handle words.

Turn the machine off.

For the next part, you will need a System Master disk and a blank disk.

1. Hold the System Master disk in your hand, with the label up and your thumb on the label. Put the disk into the disk drive—or drive #1 if you have two drives—and close the door.

2. Now turn the computer on. The disk drive will whirr and clatter. The red light will glow. Eventually the noise will stop and the red light will go out. Depending on what's inside your machine, you'll see a different message on the screen. Just ignore it for now.

3. Remove the System Master disk and substitute your blank disk. Close the door.

Type NEW, and press RETURN.

Then type INIT HELLO, and press RETURN.

The drive will whirr for a while now. What it's doing is INITializing the blank disk. This means it's arranging the disk to the Apple's particular requirements—rather like putting the company letterhead on a piece of blank stationery. You must initialize any new disk before you can use it.

4. When the noise stops and the light goes out, you can proceed to use this disk. First, let's see what's on it. Type CATALOG and press RETURN. (From here on, I'll stop reminding you about RETURN at the end of a line.) CATALOG is the command to ask what's on the disk. You can ask it at any time.

You will see:

```
DISK VOLUME 254
A   002 HELLO
```

This means you have one program, called HELLO, stored on the disk. HELLO is the initialization program. But let's make a new program.

5. Type NEW. This command is a big eraser. It rubs out anything in memory—so we have to be careful when we use it.

Type HOME. This command just clears the screen, but doesn't eliminate memory.

6. Now type the following program exactly, with a RETURN after each line. Don't worry if you don't understand it.

```
10   FOR X = 1 TO 100
20   PRINT "THIS COMPUTER IS A PUSSYCAT";
30   NEXT X
100  END
```

Look at the screen. If you've made a mistake in any line (maybe you left out the semicolon in line 20), just retype the line now. The computer will replace the old line with the new one, and arrange your instructions in numerical order before it runs it. To see that happen, type LIST. The program is now listed correctly.

7. Type RUN to run this program. Not bad—but not great.

Type LIST to list the program. You'll see your original four lines.

Let's make it more interesting, and make the machine work a little harder.

8. Type the following additional lines:

```
12  INVERSE
40  NORMAL
```

To reassure yourself that the computer has inserted these new lines in the proper place, type LIST again. You'll see:

```
10   FOR X = 1 TO 100
12   INVERSE
20   PRINT "THIS COMPUTER IS A PUSSYCAT";
30   NEXT X
40   NORMAL
100  END
```

RUN the program.

9. Type two more lines:

```
22 NORMAL
24 PRINT "                    ";
```

You'll want about fifteen spaces between the quotes. Just press the space bar. (The exact number doesn't matter.)

LIST it to see the lines have been put in correctly. Then RUN it. It's getting better, isn't it?

10. LIST it again. You'll see this:

```
10   FOR X = 1 TO 100
12   INVERSE
20   PRINT "THIS COMPUTER IS A PUSSYCAT";
22   NORMAL
24   PRINT "                    ";
30   NEXT X
40   NORMAL
100  END
```

Suppose you like this program and want to save it permanently.

11. Type SAVE PUSSYCAT.

You'll see the disk-drive light go on; it'll whirr. Your program, called

PUSSYCAT, is being SAVEd on the disk. When the red light goes out,

12. Type CATALOG. You see a new program, PUSSYCAT, has been added to the disk. It's there whenever you want it. But the same program is also still in the machine. Because disk commands such as SAVE or CATALOG don't alter the computer memory.

13. Type RUN. It still runs.
Type LIST. It still lists, so it's there.
Type CATALOG
Type PRINT 5 + 5
Type PRINT "DONALD DUCK"
Type CATALOG
Type LIST, to see that all these direct commands did not hurt the program.

This is important: the computer is like a typewriter in an office. That typewriter doesn't care if you stop typing to look up an address in a file cabinet. It doesn't even know you've stopped. In the same way, the computer doesn't know you stopped programming to check the CATALOG, or to do a little addition on the side. This is very hard to get straight: the disk and the computer memory are separate.

14. Type NEW. That'll get rid of the program.
Now type RUN, and LIST. Nothing happens, because the program was erased from memory.

But the program is still on the disk. Type CATALOG and you'll see it: PUSSYCAT.

15. To get the program back in memory, type LOAD PUSSYCAT. The disk whirrs for a while. When the cursor blinks, meaning the computer is ready, type LIST and RUN. You've got your program back.

16. Type CATALOG. Notice that PUSSYCAT is still on the disk. Just because you LOADed it into memory, you didn't erase it from the disk. You just made a copy, like a Xerox.

Right now, you have two copies of PUSSYCAT, one in memory, one on the disk.

17. LIST it. You'll see:

```
10 FOR X = 1 TO 100
12 INVERSE
20 PRINT "THIS COMPUTER IS A PUSSYCAT";
22 NORMAL
```

```
24   PRINT "
30   NEXT X
40   NORMAL
100  END
```

Now let's make some changes. Type:

```
12 FLASH
20 PRINT "YOUR NAME CONTROLS THIS PUSSYCAT";
```

But fill in your name in line 20, as in:

```
20 PRINT "DONALD DUCK CONTROLS THIS
   PUSSYCAT";
```

If you LIST it again, you'll see the computer has dutifully made the changes in the correct line numbers.

RUN it.

Depending on how long your name is, it might look better if you changed the number of spaces in line 24. Anyhow, change the number of spaces, just for fun.

LIST it after you've run it.

Let's say you like this program, too. To save it, type SAVE PUSSYCAT2. Again the disk drive whirrs.

Type CATALOG. You now see three programs: HELLO, PUSSYCAT, and PUSSYCAT2.

Turn the machine off.

Now that the machine is off, all programs in the memory are erased. But these programs are still on the disk. Take the disk out of the drive and look at it.

No change—it looks exactly the same as before.

Identify the disk by writing on the label gently with a felt-tip pen. If you don't do that with your disks, you'll get hopelessly confused.

1. Put the disk back in. Turn the machine back on.

The drive whirrs, and eventually you get a blinking cursor.

Type CATALOG.

You see your programs in the catalog. But let's make this your own personalized disk. To do that, we are going to change the HELLO program.

2. Type NEW. Then type:

```
10 REM HELLO PROGRAM
20 HOME
30 PRINT "THIS IS MY FIRST DISK"
40 PRINT CHR$(4); "CATALOG"
50 END
```

REM stands for REMark. REM means "ignore everything following the REM on this line" to the computer. And PRINT CHR$(4) is machine talk for "go to the disk and execute the following quoted command." (Don't ask why PRINT CHR$(4) is what it is. It's an arbitrary instruction set by the Apple manufacturers.)

3. Now RUN the program. It should clear the screen, and print the catalog. If it doesn't, type LIST and check it to make sure it's right. Rewrite any incorrect lines. When it works,

4. Type SAVE HELLO.
Now, there's already a program called HELLO on the disk, so you're wiping out the old HELLO program and putting in a new one. This is important. Whenever you save a program under an existing name, you obliterate the old program and replace it with a new one. We're doing it on purpose here, but it's easy to do it by accident.

5. Turn the machine off.
Turn it back on again. Not bad, huh?

6. Type LIST.
You'll see your HELLO program. The HELLO program is automatically loaded in whenever you power up with a disk, or, in computer slang, "boot" the disk.

7. Change line 30 to include your own name. To do this type:

```
30 PRINT "THIS IS DONALD DUCK'S FIRST DISK"
```

Except type your name in place of Donald's. List it to see that the change has been made.

8. RUN it to be sure the program is okay, then type SAVE HELLO. You've now modified your HELLO, and resaved it.
Turn the machine off and take a break. You're doing fine.

. . .

Now let's do one numerical problem. Turn the machine back on. We're going to convert your height from feet to centimeters. The table in my dictionary says there're 2.54 centimeters to the inch.

1. Type NEW and type HOME to clear memory and clear the screen.

Type the following program:

```
10 REM HEIGHT
20 INPUT "WHAT IS YOUR HEIGHT IN FEET,
   INCHES"; F, I
30 C = (F * 12 + I ) * 2.54
40 PRINT
50 PRINT "YOUR HEIGHT IS "; C;
   "CENTIMETERS"
60 END
```

RUN this program. Enter feet, then a comma, then inches. It works, right? If it doesn't, LIST it and check the lines to make sure they're correctly typed in.

RUN it a couple of more times, with different heights.

2. Type SAVE HEIGHT. When the disk gets through, turn the machine off.

Take a break. We're going to do just two more programs, but they'll be much more interesting.

1. Boot your disk. (Put the disk in the drive, close the door, and turn the machine on.)

2. Type NEW. Type HOME.

3. Now type the following:

```
10  REM PYRAMIDS
100 W$ = "PYRAMIDS ARE FUN"
110 FOR X = 1 TO LEN (W$) / 2
120 HTAB 20 - X
```

```
130 PRINT LEFT$(W$, X);
140 PRINT RIGHT$ (W$, X)
150 NEXT X
160 END
```

RUN this. Then list the program. Add the following lines:

```
20  HOME
100 W$ = "PYRAMID AND THE CORE THE AND
    PYRAMID"
```

RUN this. It looks better. Add the following lines.

```
30 FOR X = 1 TO 20
40 INVERSE
50 PRINT "+++++++++++++++++++++++++++++++++
   +++++"
60 NEXT X
70 NORMAL
80 VTAB 3
```

There should be 38 addition signs in line 50. Now RUN this. If you like it,

3. Type SAVE PYRAMID. Now you have it safely on the disk.

4. I have not told you how the program actually works. But you can still fiddle with it. For example:

Change the quoted words in 100 to something else, and run it. See what happens.

Change INVERSE to FLASH in line 40 and run it.

Change the background in line 50 and run it.

Change the VTAB number. Run it and see what happens.

Notice you can fool with this program in perfect safety. Even if you screw it up hopelessly, you can always LOAD PYRAMID from the disk and get back the original program off the disk.

If you stumble upon something that you like, just type SAVE PYRAMID2 or whatever you want to name it. It's your program, after all. Call it whatever you want.

Turn the machine off. Take the disk out.

We're going to do one more program—I think you'll like it, and it should amaze your friends.

Boot your disk, and when you see the cursor, type NEW, and HOME.

It's time for computer graphics. You've probably seen some computer graphics and thought they were very difficult. They aren't particularly.

You won't understand this program, but you will notice how short it is.

1. Type the following program:

```
10   REM SPIRALS
20   C = .0174
30   X1 = 140 : Y1 = 75
40   VTAB 24 : INPUT "ANGLE?"; A : N = A
50   IF A = 0 THEN TEXT : END
60   HGR
70   HCOLOR = 3
80   R = C * A : S = A / N
90   X2 = X1 + S * COS (R)
100  Y2 = Y1 - S * SIN (R)
110  ONERR GOTO 200
120  HPLOT X1,Y1 TO X2, Y2
130  A = A + N : X1 = X2 : Y1 = Y2
140  GOTO 80
200  GOTO 30
```

First, run the program a couple of times. If it doesn't work, press RESET, type LIST, and check the lines to make sure they're right.

When the program is running, I suggest you try angles of 62, 81, 102, 121. Experiment with some other values for yourself.

Notice that if you type 0 as your angle, the program quits. Type RUN to run it again.

After you've played with it a while, SAVE this program under a new name, such as SAVE SPIRALS.

If you have a color monitor, you might want to make the following changes:

```
25   H = 1
70   HCOLOR = H
131  H = H + 1 : IF H = 6 THEN H = 1
140  GOTO 70
```

And try that. If you like it, save it. But if you don't have a color monitor, just:

Call it a day.

Turn everything off, put your disk away in its jacket safely. You're done!

You've now fiddled with numbers, words, and graphics. You've learned a bit about using disks. If you decide to go further with programming, you'll find that making the machine do more complex things isn't really harder—it just takes a longer program.

If you want to pursue programming in an orderly fashion, go through your Apple Tutorial. After this session, you'll find a lot of it will be at least slightly familiar to you.

Mystery-Writer Program

The following will undoubtedly prove revolutionary and invaluable for writers everywhere. The program is written for an Apple II but can be easily modified to run on any machine.

```
10     REM   MYSTERY WRITER HELPER
11     REM
12     REM   3/82 BY MC
15     REM
20     HOME : PRINT "MYSTERY WRITER'S
       HELPER": PRINT "--------------------
       --"
30     CT = 1: REM   COUNTER
40     N = 22: REM NUMBER OF HELPFUL
       ANSWERS
50     DIM R$(50): FOR V = 1 TO N: READ
       R$(V): NEXT
60     VTAB 4: PRINT "<TYPE ANY KEY TO GET
       HELP>";: GET A$
70     X =  INT ( RND (1) * N) + 1
80     PRINT : SPEED= 150
90     VTAB 10: PRINT R$(X): SPEED= 255
110    VTAB 22: PRINT "(M)ORE OR HAD
       (E)NOUGH HELP?";: GET A$
120    IF CT = 4 THEN 160
```

```
130     IF A$ = "M" THEN CT = CT + 1: GOTO
        150
140     IF A$ = "E" THEN 170
150     VTAB 10: HTAB 1: PRINT "
                                        "
        GOTO 70
160     VTAB 10: HTAB 1: INVERSE :
        PRINT "    YOU WANT TOO MUCH HELP
          ": NORMAL
170     VTAB 23: END
180     REM
1000    REM   ---HELP---
1010    REM
1020    DATA  YOU GET KNOCKED OUT,YOU GO
        SOMEWHERE ELSE,YOU FIND A DEAD
        MAN, YOU FIND A DEAD WOMAN,YOU
        FIND A BUXOM BLONDE,SOMEONE HAS
        SEARCHED THE PLACE,A CROOKED COP
        WARNS YOU
1030    DATA YOU ARE ARRESTED, YOU FIND A
        GUN, YOU FIND A KNIFE, YOU FIND A
        FRAYED ROPE, A BULLET WHIZZES PAST
        YOUR EAR!, YOU ARE ALMOST RUN
        OVER, YOU ARE BEING FOLLOWED,YOU
        SMELL FAMILIAR PERFUME
1040    DATA THE TELEPHONE RINGS...,THERE
        IS A KNOCK AT THE DOOR,YOU HEAR
        FOOTSTEPS BEHIND YOU,YOU HEAR A
        GUNSHOT!,YOU HEAR A SCREAM!,YOU
        ARE NOT ALONE...,FORGET THIS STORY
        --IT STINKS!
```

"Computer Art"

None of the programs that follow should be taken as examples of good programming. They're not. They're all accretions, the result of starting somewhere, adding a little, taking away a little, jiggling here and there, until a desired effect is finally obtained. The point is the outcome—what you see on the screen—not how I got there.

MONDRIAN

This program creates colored blocks and lines very rapidly. The program is intended to show the range of effects possible from even the simplest slightly indeterminate program. Some combinations are attractive, and the program often gives strikingly different results from one running to the next. (If you want to stop it, just press a key.) It's easy to think that the machine is creating these patterns. But it's not creating anything—it's just following orders.

```
10    REM
20    REM    ---MONDRIAN---
30    REM     BY MC 11/81
40    REM
50    REM   S=START,F=FINISH OF SHAPE
60    REM   P1=1ST POINT,P2=2ND POINT
70    REM   L=LINE,C=COLOR,KB=KEYBOARD
      PRESS?
80    REM   DL=DELAY,DUR=# OF CYCLES
90    REM
100   TEXT : HOME
110   INVERSE : HTAB 12: PRINT "
      MONDRIAN    ": NORMAL
120   VTAB 10: INPUT "HOW LONG SHOULD IT
      RUN (1-20)?";DUR
130   VTAB 14: INPUT "HOW FAST (1-10 )?";
      DL
140   VTAB 18: INPUT "HOW DELICATELY
      (1-37)?";S
150   VTAB 23: PRINT "YOU CAN PRESS ANY
      KEY TO STOP.  NOW,"
160   VTAB 24: GOSUB 1070
170   HOME
180   GR
190   REM ----MAIN LOOP----
200   REM
210   FOR CY = 1 TO DUR
220   REM -----------
230   GOSUB 630
240   FOR L = S TO F
250   HLIN P2,P1 AT L
260   NEXT L
270   REM -----------
```

```
280   GOSUB 630
290   FOR L = S TO F
300   VLIN P2,P1 AT L
310   NEXT L
320   REM ------------
330   GOSUB 630
340   FOR L = S TO F
350   HLIN P1,P2 AT 40 - L
360   NEXT L
370   REM ------------
380   GOSUB 630
390   FOR L = S / 2 TO F
400   VLIN P1 + 1,P2 - 1 AT 40 - L
410   NEXT L
420   REM -------------
430   GOSUB 630
440   FOR L = S TO F
450   VLIN P1,P2 AT L
460   NEXT L
470   REM -------------
480   GOSUB 630
490   GOSUB 820
500   FOR L = S + 1 TO F
510   HLIN P1,P2 AT L
520   NEXT L
530   REM -------------
540   NEXT CY
550   REM -----MAIN LOOP ENDS---
560   REM
570   VTAB 24: PRINT "A)GAIN OR Q)UIT?";:
      GET A$
580   IF A$ = "A" THEN 10
590   REM
600   PRINT
610   PRINT "THE END": END
620   REM
630   REM    -----SUBROUTINES-----
640   REM
650   REM   ---KEYSTROKE?---
660   REM
670   KB = PEEK ( - 16384): IF KB > 127
      THEN POKE  - 16368,0: GOSUB 1070
680   REM
```

```
690    REM    ---RANDOM VARIABLES---
700    REM
710    C =  INT ( RND (1) * 9)
720    COLOR= C
730    F =  INT ( RND (1) * 38) + 1
740    P1 =  INT ( RND (1) * 38) + 1
750    P2 =  INT ( RND (1) * 38) + 1
760    REM
770    IF C < 5 THEN  GOSUB 920
780    IF P1 < 7 THEN  GOSUB 970
790    IF P2 > 32 THEN  GOSUB 970
800    IF F > 30 THEN  GOSUB 1020
810    REM
820    REM    -----DELAY-----
830    REM
840    D = P1 * DL
850    FOR X = 1 TO D: NEXT X
860    IF D / 2 =  INT (D / 2) THEN 880
870    RETURN
880    FOR X = 1 TO D * 2: NEXT X: RETURN
890    REM
900    REM ---ADDITIONAL SHAPES---
910    REM
920    FOR L = S TO F
930    COLOR= C / 2 + 1
940    VLIN P1,P2 AT L
950    NEXT L: RETURN
960    REM -----------
970    FOR L = S / 2 TO F
980    COLOR= (C + 1) / 2
990    HLIN P1,P2 AT 40 - L
1000   NEXT L: RETURN
1010   REM -----------
1020   FOR L = S TO F
1030   COLOR= C + 1
1040   HLIN P1,P2 AT C + C
1050   NEXT L: RETURN
1060   REM
1070   REM    ---KEYSTROKE PAUSE---
1080   REM
1090   VTAB 24: PRINT "PRESS ANY KEY TO
       CONTINUE";: GET A$
1100   FOR B = 1 TO 25: PRINT  CHR$ (8);:
```

```
              PRINT " ";: PRINT  CHR$ (8);:
              NEXT B
    1110  RETURN
```

SQUARES

Interestingly, irregularity—unexpected results—tends to make us think that creativity is occurring. SQUARES is not really so different from MONDRIAN, but it is much more orderly in its effects, and we are therefore more inclined to see the mechanical processes at work.

```
10    REM   SQUARES
20    REM
30    REM   AFTER STELLA
40    REM   BY MC 1/30/82
50    REM
60    REM   THE SQUARE IS FORMED BY
70    REM   HLIN XL,XR AT YT
80    REM   HLIN XL,XR AT YB
90    REM   VLIN YT,YB AT XL
100   REM   VLIN YT,YB AT XR
110   REM   REPEAT LOOPS FOR THICKER LINES
120   REM   COLOR=C,C+1,ETC
130   HOME
140   GR
150   REM  SET STARTING VALUES
160   C = 1
170   COLOR= C
180   XL = 19:XR = 20
190   YT = 19:YB = 20
200   GOSUB 950: REM  MAKEASQUARE
210   FOR A = 1 TO 15
220   FOR S = 1 TO 15
230   C = 1 + A
240   GOSUB 1020
250   NEXT S: NEXT A
260   REM
270   REM   ---NEXT SECTION---
280   C = 1: GOSUB 950
290   FOR A = 1 TO 15
300   FOR S = 1 TO 15
310   C = 0 + A
320   GOSUB 1020
330   S = S + 1
```

```
340   C = C + 1
350   NEXT S: NEXT A
360   REM
370   REM   ---NEXT SECTION---
380   C = 1: GOSUB 950
390   FOR A = 1 TO 15
400   FOR S = 1 TO 15
410   GOSUB 1020
420   S = S + 1
430   C = C + 1
440   GOSUB 1020
450   NEXT S: NEXT A
460   REM
470   REM   ---NEXT SECTION---
480   C = 1
490   FOR A = 1 TO 15
500   FOR S = 0 TO 15
510   C = 0 + A
520   GOSUB 1020
530   S = S + 1
540   C = C + 1
550   GOSUB 1020
560   S = S + 1
570   C = C + 1
580   NEXT S: NEXT A
590   REM
600   REM ---NEXT SECTION---
610   V = 2
620   T = 50
630   C = 1
640   FOR A = 1 TO 15
650   FOR S = 0 TO 15
660   C = 0 + A
670   FOR X = 1 TO 8
680   GOSUB 1020: GOSUB 1100
690   NEXT X
700   GOSUB 1020
710   NEXT S: NEXT A
720   REM
730   REM   THE SAME WITH SPACING CHANGE
740   C = 0
750   FOR A = 1 TO 5
760   FOR S = 0 TO 15
```

```
770     GOSUB 1020
780     NEXT S: NEXT A
790     REM
800     REM  ---NEXT PART---
810     REM
820     V = 1:C = 1
830     FOR A = 1 TO 15
840     FOR S = 0 TO 15
850     C = 0 + A
860     FOR X = 1 TO 2
870     GOSUB 1020: GOSUB 1100
880     FOR TM = 1 TO 50: NEXT TM
890     NEXT X
900     NEXT S: NEXT A
910     REM
920     END
930     REM  ----SUBROUTINES---
940     REM
950     REM  MAKE A SQUARE
960     HLIN XL,XR AT YT
970     HLIN XL,XR AT YB
980     VLIN YT,YB AT XL
990     VLIN YT,YB AT XR
1000    RETURN
1010    REM
1020    REM  MAKE ANOTHER SQUARE
1030    COLOR= C + 1
1040    HLIN XL - S,XR + S AT YT - S
1050    HLIN XL - S,XR + S AT YB + S
1060    VLIN YT - S,YB + S AT XL - S
1070    VLIN YT - S,YB + S AT XR + S
1080    RETURN
1090    REM
1100    REM  ADD COUNTER
1110    S = S + V
1120    C = C + 1
1130    RETURN
```

BLACKIE

This program plays field/ground tricks. It uses the Applesoft SCRN function to search for areas of color, or lack of color. It's chiefly of interest when compared to FLAG.

```
10    REM    ---BLACKIE---
20    REM
30    REM   BY MC 11/81
40    REM
50    HOME : GR :C = 1: FOR CY = 1 TO 300:
      COLOR= C:X =   INT ( RND (1) * 37)
60    Y =   INT ( RND (1) * 37): IF   SCRN
      (X, Y) = 0 THEN   GOSUB 120
70    C = C + 1: IF  C > 12 THEN C = 1
80    NEXT : COLOR= 0: FOR CY = 1 TO 200:X
      =   INT ( RND (1) * 39):Y =    INT
      ( RND (1) * 39)
90    IF   SCRN( X,Y) = 0 THEN   HLIN 0,39
      AT Y
100   X =   INT ( RND (1) * 39):Y =   INT
      ( RND (1) * 39): IF   SCRN( X,Y) = 0
      THEN VLIN 0,39 AT X
110   FOR X = 1 TO 50: NEXT : NEXT : FOR
      Y = 0 TO 39: HLIN 0,39 AT Y: NEXT :
      END
120   REM   SQUARE
130   FOR Y = Y TO Y + 3: HLIN X,X + 3 AT
      Y: NEXT : RETURN
```

FLAG

This is an example of a fake program. At first glance, it appears to shift red, white, and blue rectangles around on the screen to create an American flag. (This effect is much more striking if the program is compiled; the program as written runs rather slowly.)

But actually, FLAG is doing nothing of the sort. It's just laying down a random pattern of red, white, and blue spots, and then overprinting a flag on the original pattern.

To see what it's really doing, skip over the original pattern by adding this line:

```
45 A = 1 : B = 15 : C = 2 : GR : GOTO
   110
```

There are many ways to instruct the machine to make a flag. The method here is the only way I knew at the time.

```
10    REM    -----FLAG---
20    REM
30    REM       11/81
40    HOME
50    A = 1:B = 15:C = 2: GR : FOR X = 0
      TO 39: FOR Y = 0 TO 38:R =   INT
      ( RND (1) * 3) + 1
60    ON R GOTO 70,80,90
70    COLOR= A: GOTO 100
80    COLOR= B: GOTO 100
90    COLOR= C: GOTO 100
100   PLOT X,Y: NEXT : NEXT : REM   SCAN
110   REM
120   FOR Z = 5 TO 1 STEP  - 2: FOR Y = 0
      TO 38 STEP Z + 1: FOR X = 0 TO 39
      STEP Z + 1
130   GOSUB 330: NEXT : NEXT : FOR X = 0
      TO 39 STEP Z: FOR Y = 0 TO 38
      STEP Z
140   GOSUB 330: NEXT : NEXT : NEXT
150   REM   RED=A,WH=B,BL=C
160   A = 1:B = 15:C = 2: GOSUB 470:
      GOSUB 550:A = 15:B = 1:C = 2: GOSUB
      470: GOSUB 550
170   A = 15:B = 2:C = 1: GOSUB 470:
      GOSUB 550:A = 2:B = 15:C = 1: GOSUB
      470: GOSUB 550
180   A = 2:B = 1:C = 15: GOSUB 470:
      GOSUB 550:A = 1:B = 2:C = 15: GOSUB
      470: GOSUB 550
190   REM   MAKE COMPLEMENTARY
200   REM   RED=A,WH=B,BL=C
210   A = 4:B = 0:C = 9: GOSUB 470: GOSUB
      550: GOSUB 550:A = 4:B = 9:C = 0
220   GOSUB 470: FOR X = 1 TO 500: NEXT :
      A = 4:B = 0:C = 0: GOSUB 470: FOR
      X = 1 TO 500: NEXT X
230   A = 0:B = 0:C = 0: GOSUB 470: REM
      MAKE PALE
240   A = 11:B = 15:C = 7: GOSUB 470:
      GOSUB 550: REM   BLACK COMBOS
250   A = 0:B = 5:C = 15: GOSUB 470:
      GOSUB 550:A = 15:B = 0:C = 5: GOSUB
      470: GOSUB 550
```

```
260    A = 15:B = 7:C = 5: GOSUB 470:
       GOSUB 550:A = 11:B = 15:C = 5:
       GOSUB 470: GOSUB 550
270    REM   ALL BLUE
280    A = 6:B = 2:C = 6: GOSUB 470: GOSUB
       550:A = 4:B = 6:C = 9: GOSUB 470:
       GOSUB 550
290    A = 1:B = 3:C = 9: GOSUB 470: GOSUB
       550:A = 5:B = 15:C = 9: GOSUB 470:
       GOSUB 550
300    A = 1:B = 15:C = 2: GOSUB 470:
       GOSUB 550:A = 1:B = 0:C = 2: GOSUB
       470: GOSUB 550
310    A = 1:B = 0:C = 0: GOSUB 470: GOSUB
       550:A = 0:B = 0:C = 0: GOSUB 470
320    END
330    REM   PLOT A FLAG
340    REM   BLUE BG
350    IF (X = 0 OR X = 2 OR X = 4 OR X =
       6 OR X = 8 OR X = 10 OR X = 12 OR
       X = 14 OR X = 16) AND Y < 21 THEN
       460
360    IF (X = 1 OR X = 3 OR X = 5 OR X =
       7 OR X = 9 OR X = 11 OR X = 13 OR
       X = 15) AND (Y = 0 OR Y = 1 OR Y =
       3 OR Y = 4 OR Y = 6 OR Y = 7 OR Y =
       9 OR Y = 10 OR Y = 12 OR Y = 13 OR
       Y = 15 OR Y = 16 OR Y = 18 OR Y =
       19 OR Y = 20) THEN 460
370    IF X > 16 AND (Y = 3 OR Y = 4 OR Y =
       5 OR Y = 9 OR Y = 10 OR Y = 11 OR
       Y = 15 OR Y = 16 OR Y = 17) THEN
       440
380    IF Y = 21 OR Y = 22 OR Y = 23 OR Y =
       27 OR Y = 28 OR Y = 29 OR Y = 33
       OR Y = 34 OR Y = 35 THEN 440
390    REM   RED STRIPES
400    IF X > 16 AND (Y = 0 OR Y = 1 OR Y =
       2 OR Y = 6 OR Y = 7 OR Y = 8 OR Y =
       12 OR Y = 13 OR Y = 14 OR Y = 18
       OR Y = 19 OR Y = 20) THEN 450
410    IF Y = 24 OR Y = 25 OR Y = 26 OR Y =
       30 OR Y = 31 OR Y = 32 OR Y = 36
       OR Y = 37 OR Y = 38 THEN 450
```

```
420    IF (X = 1 OR X = 3 OR X = 5 OR X =
       7 OR X = 9 OR X = 11 OR X = 13 OR
       X = 15) AND (Y = 2 OR Y = 5 OR Y =
       8 OR Y = 11 OR Y = 14 OR Y = 17)
       THEN 440
430    COLOR= 0: RETURN
440    COLOR= B: PLOT X,Y: RETURN
450    COLOR= A: PLOT X,Y: RETURN
460    COLOR= C: PLOT X,Y: RETURN
470    REM   MAKE A FLAG
480    REM   SET STRIPES
490    COLOR= A: FOR S = 0 TO 39 STEP 6:
       FOR Y = S TO S + 2: HLIN 0,39 AT Y:
       NEXT : NEXT
500    REM   SET OTHER STRIPES
510    COLOR= B: FOR S = 3 TO 36 STEP 6:
       FOR Y = S TO S + 2: HLIN 0,39 AT Y:
       NEXT : NEXT
520    REM   BACKGROUND
530    COLOR= C: FOR Y = 0 TO 20: HLIN
       0,17 AT Y: NEXT
540    COLOR= B: FOR X = 1 TO 16 STEP 2:
       FOR Y = 2 TO 18 STEP 3: PLOT X,Y:
       NEXT : NEXT : RETURN
550    FOR X = 1 TO 1000: NEXT X: RETURN
```

Non-Rational Programs

Computers can be used for almost anything. I'm interested in the I Ching, an ancient Chinese method of telling the future. My I CHING program, with comments, an explanation of how the program works, and suggestions for modifications, originally appeared in *Creative Computing,* March, 1983. The version included here has been modified to make it more easily adapted to other machines.

How the I Ching works—and whether it works at all—is an interesting speculation. The Chinese text is wise in any case. I find the I Ching valuable, although I have no interest in astrology and other divination techniques.

The method by which the I Ching arrives at an answer is quite complicated. It's natural to wonder whether the method has real power, or whether we will derive meaning from any reasonably cryptic answer to our questions. To get a sense of the extent to which we tend to supply our own meanings, I wrote SOOTHSAYER.

SOOTHSAYER is extremely simple, as simple as MYSTERY WRITER. The program selects an answer at random to your question, and thus it might be thought of as a control for the I Ching. This depends on your concept of chance and random events. If you have any sympathy for ideas such as Jung's notion of synchronicity, you will tend to see both the I CHING and SOOTHSAYER as subject to unexplained controlling influences of a similar sort. That would make SOOTHSAYER merely a not very wise version of the I CHING. Similarly, if you think this Eastern mysticism is all mumbo jumbo, then both programs will be perceived as mumbo jumbo in the same way.

Yet from one standpoint it seems to me that these programs have indisputable value. We all have unconscious thoughts that influence our perceptions and behavior to a far greater degree than we care to admit. It seems worthwhile to bring these influences to conscious awareness by any means possible. For that reason alone, the programs—and our reactions to them—are worth our attention.

```
10    REM        I CHING (REVISED)
12    REM
13    REM    ----------------------
14    REM    THIS PROGRAM THROWS &
16    REM    LOOKS UP HEXAGRAMS
18    REM    AND ALSO GENERATES
19    REM    SECONDARY AND NUCLEAR
20    REM    HEXAGRAMS
22    REM    ----------------------
23    REM
24    REM    COMPLETED 9/23/82
25    REM    SIMPLIFIED 12/12/83
26    REM    BY MICHAEL CRICHTON
28    REM
50    REM    **** INITIALIZATION ***
51    REM
52    REM    T= LOOKUP TABLE, R$=RESPONSES
55    DIM T(8,8): FOR V = 1 TO 8: FOR H =
      1 TO 8: READ T (V,H): NEXT H,V
56    DIM R$(64): FOR V = 1 TO 64: READ
      R$(V): NEXT V
99    REM
```

```
100   REM     **** FIRST OPTIONS ***
110   REM
120   HOME : TEXT
130   VTAB 8: HTAB 10: INVERSE : PRINT
      "  I CHING PROGRAM  ": NORMAL :
      VTAB 11: HTAB 18: PRINT "BY": VTAB
      14: HTAB 11: PRINT "MICHAEL
      CRICHTON"
140   VTAB 22: PRINT "(I)INSTRUCTIONS,
      (C)OINS, OR (M)ACHINE  INPUT?  ";:
      GET A$
150   IF A$ = "I" GOTO 6000: REM  INSTR
160   IF A$ = "C" GOTO 200: REM  COINS
170   IF A$ = "M" GOTO 300: REM  MACHINE
      INPUT
180   REM
200   REM    **** COIN INPUT ****
201   REM
210   HOME :PS = 18
220   VTAB 8: PRINT "TOSS COINS SIX
      TIMES..."
230   FOR I = 1 TO 6
240   VTAB (PS) : INPUT L(I)
250   IF L(I) < 6 OR L(I) > 9 THEN  VTAB
      (PS): PRINT "    VALUE
      UNACCEPTABLE": GOTO 240
260   REM POKE 780 + I,L
270   PS = PS - 1: NEXT I
280   GOTO 600
290   REM
300   REM    **** MACHINE INPUT ****
301   REM
310   HOME :PS = 18
320   VTAB 8: PRINT "PRESS  KEYBOARD SIX
      TIMES..."
330   FOR I = 1 TO 6
340   CH =  INT ( RND (1) * 100)
345   REM  FIRST "COIN"
350   X =  INT ( RND (1) * CH)
360   IF X / 2 =  INT (X / 2)  THEN C1 =
      2: GOTO 380
370   C1 = 3
380   REM NEXT "COIN"
390   X =  INT ( RND (1) * CH)
```

```
400   IF X / 2 =  INT (X / 2) THEN C2 = 2:
      GOTO 420
410   C2 = 3
420   REM NEXT "COIN"
430   X =  INT ( RND (1) * CH)
440   IF X / 2 =  INT (X / 2) THEN C3 = 2:
      GOTO 460
450   C3 = 3
460   REM
480   REM  KEYBOARD PRESSED?
485   REM
490   KB =   PEEK ( - 16384): IF KB > 127
      THEN  POKE  - 16368,0: GOTO 520
500   GOTO 340: REM  BEGIN ANOTHER PASS
510   REM
520   REM  KEYBOARD WAS PRESSED
525   REM
530   L(I) = C1 + C2 + C3: VTAB (PS):
      PRINT L(I)
550   PS = PS - 1: NEXT I
555   PRINT  CHR$ (7): REM WARNING BEEP
560   REM
600   REM   **** BEGIN PROCESSING ***
610   REM
620   VTAB 12: PRINT "HEXAGRAM COMPLETED":
      FOR DL = 1 TO 500: NEXT
630   HOME
640   Y = 18
650   VTAB (Y)
660   FOR I = 1 TO 6
670   L = L(I): GOSUB 2000
675   Y = Y - 3
680   NEXT I
699   REM
700   REM    *** READ ANSWER ***
705   REM
710   L1$ =  STR$ (L(1)):L2$ =  STR$
      (L(2)):L3$ =  STR$ (L(3)):L4$ =
      STR$ (L(4)): L5$ =  STR$ (L(5)):L6$
      =  STR$ (L(6))
730   LT$ = L1$ + L2$ + L3$:UT$ = L4$ +
      L5$ + L6$: REM LOWER/UPPER TRIGRAMS
740   T1$ = LT$: GOSUB 2200: GOSUB 3000
```

```
750     LT = TM
760     T1$ = UT$: GOSUB 2200: GOSUB 3000
770     UT = TM
780     H1 = T(LT,UT): REM PRIMARY HEXAGRAM
        VAL
790     VTAB 22: PRINT " # ";H1;"    ";
        R$(H1)
800     FOR DL = 1 TO 500: NEXT DL
810     VTAB 24: PRINT " LINES ARE:   ";L1$;
        "-";L2$;"-";L3$;"-";L4$;"-";L5$;"-";
        L6$;"    ";: GET A$
820     REM    *** OTHER TRIGRAMS ***
830     REM   SECONDARY TRIGRAM
840     T2$ = LT$: GOSUB 2300: GOSUB 3000:
        LT = TM
850     T2$ = UT$: GOSUB 2300: GOSUB 3000:
        UT = TM
860     H2 = T(LT,UT): REM H2=2NDARY
        HEXAGRAM VAL
870     REM    FIRST NUCLEAR
880     LN$ = L2$ + L3$ + L4$:UN$ = L3$ +
        L4$ + L5$
890     T1$ = LN$: GOSUB 2200: GOSUB 3000:
        LN = TM
900     T1$ = UN$: GOSUB 2200: GOSUB 3000:
        UN = TM
910     N1 = T(LN,UN): REM   NUCLEAR 1 HEX
        VAL
920     REM    SECOND NUCLEAR
930     T2$ = LN$: GOSUB 2300: GOSUB 3000:
        LN = TM
940     T2$ = UN$: GOSUB 2300: GOSUB 3000:
        UN = TM
950     N2 = T(LN,UN): REM   NUCLEAR 2 HEX
        VAL
960     REM
1270    REM
1280    TEXT : HOME
1290    PRINT "CASTING WAS:   ";L1$;"-";L2$;
        "-";L3$;"-";L4$;"-";L5$;"-";L6$
1300    PRINT "----------------------------
        -----------": PRINT
1310    PRINT "PRIMARY HEXAGRAM-": PRINT
```

```
1320   HTAB 6: PRINT H1;"   ";R$(H1):
       PRINT
1330   PRINT "SECONDARY HEXAGRAM-": PRINT
1340   HTAB 6: PRINT H2;"   ";R$(H2):
       PRINT
1350   PRINT "FIRST NUCLEAR-": PRINT
1360   HTAB 6: PRINT N1;"   ";R$(N1):
       PRINT
1370   PRINT "SECOND NUCLEAR-": PRINT
1380   HTAB 6: PRINT N2;"   ";R$(N2)
1400   :
1410   IF PX = 1 THEN  PRINT : PRINT
       CHR$ (4);"PR#0": GOTO 1500
1411   REM
1415   REM   ----PRINT ROUTINE---
1416   REM
1420   PRINT : PRINT : PRINT "DO YOU WANT
       A PRINTOUT (Y/N)?";: GET A$
1430   FOR B = 1 TO 29: PRINT  CHR$ (8);:
       PRINT " ";: PRINT  CHR$ (8);: NEXT
       B
1440   IF A$ = "N" GOTO 1500
1450   PX = 1: INPUT "TODAY'S DATE
       (MM/DD/YY)?";D$
1460   FOR B = 1 TO 40: PRINT  CHR$ (8);:
       PRINT " ";: PRINT  CHR$ (8);: NEXT
       B
1470   PRINT "WHAT WAS YOUR QUESTION?":
       INPUT Q$: PRINT  CHR$ (4);"PR#1":
       PRINT : PRINT D$;"   ";Q$: PRINT
1490   GOTO 1290
1500   END
1510   REM
1998   REM   **** START SUBROUTINES ***
1999   REM
2000   REM *** DRAW GRAPHIC ****
2001   REM
2004   VTAB (Y): HTAB 5
2005   INVERSE
2010   IF L = 6 THEN  PRINT  SPC( 10);:
       NORMAL : PRINT  SPC( 5);: INVERSE :
       PRINT  SPC( 10): NORMAL : RETURN
2020   IF L = 7 THEN  PRINT  SPC( 25):
       NORMAL : RETURN
2030   IF L = 8 THEN  PRINT  SPC ( 10);:
```

```
          NORMAL : PRINT  SPC( 5);: INVERSE :
          PRINT  SPC( 10): NORMAL : RETURN
2040   IF L = 9 THEN  PRINT  SPC( 25):
          NORMAL : RETURN
2050   REM
2100   REM *** 2NDARY HEX CONVERSION
2105   REM
2110   IF L = 6 THEN L = 7: RETURN
2120   IF L = 9 THEN L = 8: RETURN
2130   REM
2200   REM *** CONVERT TRIGRAM #'S  FOR
          LOOKUP ***
2205   REM
2210   S$ = "":X$ = "": REM  NULL
2220   FOR N = 1 TO  LEN (T1$)
2230   X$ =  MID$ (T1$,N,1)
2240   IF X$ = "6" THEN X$ ="8"
2250   IF X$ = "9" THEN X$ = "7"
2260   S$ = S$ + X$: NEXT N
2270   T1$ = S$: RETURN
2280   REM
2300   REM  *** CONVERT OTHER TRIGRAMS
          ***
2305   REM
2310   S$ = "":X$ = "": REM  NULL
2320   FOR N = 1 TO  LEN (T2$)
2330   X$ =  MID$ (T2$,N,1)
2340   IF X$ = "6" THEN X$ = "7"
2350   IF X$ = "9" THEN X$ = "8"
2360   S$ = S$ + X$: NEXT N
2370   T1$ = S$: RETURN
2380   REM
3000   REM *** CONVERT 1-8 ****
3005   REM
3010   TM =  VAL (T1$)
3020   IF TM = 777 THEN TM = 1: GOTO 3100
3030   IF TM = 788 THEN TM = 2: GOTO 3100
3040   IF TM = 878 THEN TM = 3: GOTO 3100
3050   IF TM = 887 THEN TM = 4: GOTO 3100
3060   IF TM = 888 THEN TM = 5: GOTO 3100
3070   IF TM = 877 THEN TM = 6: GOTO 3100
3080   IF TM = 787 THEN TM = 7: GOTO 3100
3090   IF TM = 778 THEN TM = 8
```

```
3100   RETURN
3110   REM
3500   REM    *** LOOKUP TABLE DATA ***
3510   REM
3520   DATA   1,34,5,26,11,9,14,43
3530   DATA   25,51,3,27,24,42,21,17
3540   DATA   6,40,29,4,7,59,64,47
3550   DATA   33,62,39,52,15,53,56,31
3560   DATA   12,16,8,23,2,20,35,45
3570   DATA   44,32,48,18,46,57,50,28
3580   DATA   13,55,63,22,36,37,30,49
3590   DATA   10,54,60,41,19,61,38,58
3595   REM
4000   REM    *** RESPONSE DATA ***
4010   REM
4020   DATA   THE CREATIVE
4030   DATA   THE RECEPTIVE
4040   DATA   DIFFICULT BEGINNINGS
4050   DATA   YOUTHFUL FOLLY
       (INEXPERIENCE)
4060   DATA   CALCULATED WAITING
4070   DATA   CONFLICT
4080   DATA   THE ARMY
4090   DATA   HOLDING TOGETHER
4100   DATA   THE TAMING POWER OF THE
       SMALL
4110   DATA   RESTRAINED CONDUCT
       (TREADING)
4120   DATA   PEACE
4130   DATA   STAGNATION
4140   DATA   FELLOWSHIP WITH MEN
4150   DATA   POSSESSION IN GREAT MEASURE
4160   DATA   MODESTY (MODERATION)
4170   DATA   ENTHUSIASM
4180   DATA   FOLLOWING
4190   DATA   WORK ON WHAT HAS BEEN
       SPOILED
4200   DATA   APPROACH
4210   DATA   CONTEMPLATION
4220   DATA   BITING THROUGH
4230   DATA   GRACE
4240   DATA   DETERIORATION (SPLITTING
       APART)
```

```
4250   DATA   RETURN
4260   DATA   INNOCENCE
4270   DATA   THE TAMING POWER OF THE
              GREAT
4280   DATA   NOURISHMENT
4290   DATA   PREPONDERANCE OF THE GREAT
4300   DATA   THE ABYSMAL (DANGER)
4310   DATA   THE CLINGING
4320   DATA   ATTRACTION
4330   DATA   ENDURING
4340   DATA   RETREAT
4350   DATA   THE POWER OF THE GREAT
4360   DATA   PROGRESS
4370   DATA   DARKENING OF THE LIGHT
4380   DATA   THE FAMILY
4390   DATA   OPPOSITION
4400   DATA   OBSTRUCTION
4410   DATA   DELIVERANCE (LIBERATION)
4420   DATA   DECREASE
4430   DATA   INCREASE
4440   DATA   RESOLUTION
4450   DATA   COMING TO MEET (TEMPTATION)
4460   DATA   GATHERING TOGETHER
4470   DATA   PUSHING UPWARD
4480   DATA   OPPRESSION
4490   DATA   THE SOURCE (THE WELL)
4500   DATA   REVOLUTION
4510   DATA   THE CALDRON
4520   DATA   AROUSING (SHOCK)
4530   DATA   KEEPING STILL
4540   DATA   DEVELOPMENT
4550   DATA   THE MARRYING MAIDEN
4560   DATA   ABUNDANCE
4570   DATA   TRAVELLING
4580   DATA   GENTLE INFLUENCE
4590   DATA   JOY
4600   DATA   DISPERSION
4610   DATA   LIMITATIONS
4620   DATA   INNER TRUTH
4630   DATA   PREPONDERANCE OF THE SMALL
4640   DATA   AFTER COMPLETION
4650   DATA   BEFORE COMPLETION
4660   :
4670   :
```

```
6000   REM   ***INSTRUCTIONS***
6010   HOME
6020   PRINT "THE I CHING IS AN ANCIENT
       CHINESE METHOD OF DIVINATION. BY
       REPEATEDLY THROWING STICKS OR
       COINS, A SIX-LINE FIGURE, OR
       HEXAGRAM, IS CREATED."
6030   PRINT
6040   PRINT "THIS HEXAGRAM IS
       INTERPRETED  BY CONSULTING A
       METAPHORICAL TEXT."
6050   PRINT
6060   PRINT "FURTHER INFORMATION CAN BE
       OBTAINED  BY DERIVING A SECONDARY
       HEXAGRAM, AND TWO  SO-CALLED
       'NUCLEAR HEXAGRAMS'. "
6070   PRINT
6080   PRINT "THIS PROGRAM PROVIDES THE
       HEXAGRAM NAMESONLY.  FOR FURTHER
       INTERPRETATION, USERSSHOULD OBTAIN
       A   GOOD I CHING TEXT, SUCHAS THE
       CLASSIC TRANSLATION BY RICHARD
       WILHELM (PRINCETON UNIVERSITY
       PRESS)."
6090   GOSUB 8000
6100   HOME : PRINT "CASTING THE I CHING"
6110   PRINT : INVERSE : PRINT "WITH
       COINS": NORMAL
6120   PRINT
6130   PRINT "USE THREE SIMILAR COINS,
       SUCH AS PENNIES. ASSIGN ONE FACE
       THE VALUE OF 3,AND THE OTHER FACE
       THE VALUE OF 2. THINKON YOUR
       QUESTION AS YOU CAST THE COINS
       SIX TIMES."
6140   PRINT
6150   PRINT "AFTER EACH THROW, SUM THE
       THREE FACES, TO GET A VALUE FROM 6
       TO 9. ENTER THIS VALUE INTO THE
       COMPUTER."
6160   PRINT : PRINT : INVERSE : PRINT "
       BY COMPUTER ": NORMAL : PRINT
6170   PRINT
6180   PRINT "THE COMPUTER WILL SIMULATE
```

```
            COIN TOSSES   IF YOU PRESS ANY KEY
            SIX TIMES."
6190    GOSUB 8000
6200    HOME : PRINT "INTERPRETING THE I
            CHING": PRINT : PRINT
6210    PRINT "THE COMPUTER FIRST
            GENERATES THE PRIMARYHEXAGRAM.":
            PRINT
6220    PRINT : PRINT
6230    PRINT "IT WILL THEN ADD THE
            HEXAGRAM NAME, AND THE LINE VALUES
            READING FROM BOTTOM TO TOP.":
            PRINT
6240    PRINT
6290    PRINT "<RETURN> WILL SUMMARIZE THE
            DATA ON ALL FOUR HEXAGRAMS, AND
            PROVIDE A PRINTOUT  OPTION."
6300    GOTO 140
6310    REM
7998    REM   ***PAUSE***
7999    REM
8000    VTAB 24: PRINT "PRESS ANY KEY TO
            CONTINUE";: GET A$: RETURN
```

```
10      REM      SOOTHSAYER
20      REM
30      REM      ---------------------
40      REM
50      REM      COMPLETED 10/23/82
60      REM      BY MICHAEL CRICHTON
70      REM
80      REM      **** INITIALIZATION ***
90      REM
110     DIM R$(64): FOR V = 1 TO 64: READ
        R$(V): NEXT V
120     REM
150     HOME : TEXT
160     VTAB 8: HTAB 7: INVERSE : PRINT
        "SOOTHSAYER": NORMAL: VTAB 11: HTAB
        18: PRINT "BY": VTAB 14: HTAB 11:
        PRINT "MICHAEL CRICHTON"
170     VTAB 22: HTAB 7: PRINT "PRESS ANY
        KEY TO BEGIN";: GET A$
180     REM
200     REM      **** BEGIN INPUT ****
210     REM
220     HOME
230     VTAB 8: PRINT "WHAT IS YOUR
        QUESTION:"
240     PRINT : INPUT Q$
245     IF   LEN (Q$) < 8 THEN  VTAB 14:
        PRINT "SORRY, DIDN'T HEAR THAT...":
        GOTO 330
250     REM
260     REM   *** MAKE RESPONSE ***
270     REM
280     V =    INT ( RND (1) * 64) + 1
300     SPEED= 100
310     VTAB 14: PRINT R$(V)
320     SPEED= 255
330     VTAB 22
340     PRINT "DO YOU WISH TO ASK ANOTHER":
        PRINT "QUESTION (Y/N)?";: GET A$
350     IF A$ = "N" THEN 380
355     GOTO 180
360     REM
370     REM      *** ENDING ***
380     HOME
```

```
390   VTAB 8: PRINT "THE CONSULTATION IS
      AT AN END.": PRINT : PRINT "LIVE
      AND PROSPER IN THE KNOWLEDGE":
      PRINT "THAT MY ANSWERS ARE TOTALLY
      RANDOM"
400   END
410   REM
420   REM  **** DATA ENTRIES ****
430   REM
440   DATA  ONE CAN KNOW GOOD ONLY
      BECAUSE THERE IS EVIL
450   DATA  THE MIND IS FULL OF QUESTIONS
      BUT THE HEART KNOWS ALL
460   DATA  NOT COLLECTING TREASURES
      PREVENTS STEALING
470   DATA  BE STILL
480   DATA  HOLD FAST TO THE CENTER
490   DATA  EASY COME EASY GO
500   DATA  HEAVEN AND HELL ARE BOTH
      WITHIN
510   DATA  A GREAT TAILOR CUTS LITTLE.
520   DATA  PRACTICE RESTRAINT
530   DATA  TAKE CARE OF ALL THINGS AND
      ABANDON NOTHING
540   DATA  TO BE RESTLESS IS TO LOSE
      ONE'S CONTROL
550   DATA  HE WHO DOES NOT TRUST ENOUGH
      WILL NOT BE TRUSTED
560   DATA  RETIRE WHEN THE WORK IS DONE
570   DATA  THROUGH SELFLESS ACTION YOU
      WILL ATTAIN FULFILLMENT
580   DATA  ACCEPT MISFORTUNE AS THE
      HUMAN CONDITION
590   DATA  EMPTY YOURSELF OF ALL
      DESIRES
600   DATA  GIVE UP LEARNING AND PUT AN
      END TO YOUR TROUBLES
610   DATA  UNDERSTANDING IS THE BOOBY
      PRIZE
620   DATA  WE SEE THE WORLD AS WE KNOW
      IT TO BE
630   DATA  HE THAT CAN HAVE PATIENCE CAN
      HAVE EVERYTHING
640   DATA  HE WHO MAKES A SHOW IS NOT
```

```
      ENLIGHTENED
650   DATA   ONE CAN ALWAYS DEPEND ON THE
      KINDNESS OF STRANGERS
660   DATA   PRIDE GOETH BEFORE A FALL
670   DATA   ALL THAT YOU SEEK LIES WITHIN
      YOURSELF
680   DATA   WEAPONS ARE NOT THE TOOLS OF
      THE WISE
690   DATA   HE WHO KNOWS HE HAS ENOUGH IS
      RICH
700   DATA   ROLL WITH THE PUNCHES
710   DATA   CHANGE COMES WITH STILLNESS
720   DATA   INACTION IS A FORM OF ACTION
730   DATA   SEE WHAT IS REAL AND NOT WHAT
      IS APPARENT
740   DATA   TOO MUCH SUCCESS IS NOT AN
      ADVANTAGE
750   DATA   AS YOU LIVE SO SHALL YOU DIE
760   DATA   THE PAST IS FATHER OF THE
      FUTURE
770   DATA   A CONTENTED MAN IS NEVER
      DISAPPOINTED
780   DATA   GREAT INTELLIGENCE SOMETIMES
      SEEMS STUPID
790   DATA   THERE ARE NO INNOCENT VICTIMS
800   DATA   DISAPPOINTMENT SPRINGS FROM
      DESIRE
810   DATA   KEEP YOUR MOUTH SHUT AND YOU
      WILL LEARN PEACE
820   DATA   BE SIMPLE AND BE FREE
830   DATA   HAPPINESS SPRINGS FROM MISERY
      AND MISERY FROM HAPPINESS.  IT IS
      ALWAYS SO.
840   DATA   HOWEVER GOOD OR BAD IT WILL
      SOON CHANGE
850   DATA   WHY DOES THE BLIND MAN'S WIFE
      PAINT HER FACE?
860   DATA   YOU CAN BE TOO CLEVER FOR
      YOUR OWN GOOD
870   DATA   BLISS FOLLOWS DETACHMENT FROM
      WORLDLY DESIRES
880   DATA   YOU WORRY ABOUT TRIVIAL
      MATTERS
890   DATA   LIFE IS HARD
```

```
900    DATA  YOU CAN'T GET ENOUGH OF WHAT
       YOU DON'T NEED.
910    DATA  HOW MANY PSYCHIATRISTS DOES
       IT TAKE TO CHANGE A LIGHTBULB?  ONE
       --BUT THE LIGHTBULB HAS TO WANT TO
       CHANGE.
920    DATA  ASK YOURSELF HOW YOU HAVE
       GOTTEN TO THIS STATE.
930    DATA  MEDITATE ON FREEDOM FROM CARE
940    DATA  WHEN IN DOUBT THROW IT OUT
950    DATA  SEE THE GOOD IN ALL THINGS
960    DATA  YOU KNOW YOUR QUESTIONS ARE
       EXTREMELY IRRITATING.  WHY DON'T
       YOU PULL YOURSELF TOGETHER AND DEAL
       WITH YOUR OWN PROBLEMS?
970    DATA  MAN DOES NOT LIVE BY BREAD
       ALONE
980    DATA  MOST PEOPLE FIND WHAT THEY
       ARE LOOKING FOR--THAT'S THE
       PROBLEM.
990    DATA  MOVE SLOWLY AND SEE
1000   DATA  RISK ALL AND GAIN EVERYTHING
1010   DATA  ASK HOW YOU HAVE CONTRIBUTED
       TO OR CAUSED THIS SITUATION
1020   DATA  LIFE IS A FATAL DISEASE.  NO
       ONE SURVIVES IT.
1030   DATA  LIVE IN THE MOMENT
1040   DATA  SEE YOUR WAKING HOURS AS A
       DREAM
1050   DATA  YOU ALREADY KNOW THE ANSWER
1060   DATA  THE RIVER RUNS FULL IN THE
       SPRING AND DRY IN THE FALL
1070   DATA  ALL THINGS END IN THEIR OWN
       TIME
1080   DATA  FORTUNE AND MISFORTUNE ARE
       FACES ON THE SAME COIN
```

IBM APPENDIX

Taking Charge of an IBM Personal Computer

The following routine can be done in two hours. You will need an IBM Personal Computer with two disk drives, a DOS disk, and a blank disk.

You'll be entering programs, but I won't usually explain them. Don't let this worry you. Just type them in. The whole point is to show you what you don't need to understand.

Let's get started.

1. Without putting a disk in the drive, turn the computer on. (The switch is at the rear right side of the machine.)

After a short pause when nothing seems to happen, the screen will glow and the empty disk drive will clatter for a moment. Pretty soon you'll see a blinking dash on the upper left screen. This is the cursor: it means the machine is awaiting your instructions. So let's give it some instructions and show it who's boss.

2. At the keyboard, type PRINT 5 + 5. You will see this appear on the screen as you type. If you make a mistake in typing, just move the cursor back, using the arrow key, and retype it correctly.

You'll eventually have PRINT 5 + 5 on the screen, but nothing further happens. So press the carriage-return key. (This key has a backward "L" and an arrow on it; we'll call it CR.) The return key means "enter this instruction into the computer."

Instantly, you see "10" on the next line. This is encouraging—the stupid machine got it right.

3. Now type PRINT 5 * 5, and press CR. (The * means "multiply.")
You receive a gratifyingly quick answer of "25." Try PRINT 5 − 5, and
then PRINT 5 / 5. (The / means to "divide by.") Notice the machine
consistently obeys you. But perhaps you feel it's too quick—maybe we
should slow it down a little.

4. Type PRINT 5.01 * 5.02 − 5.03 / 2.04 * 100.05 + 3.06 + 20.07
− 200.08 + 300.09 / 1.10. Make sure you're hitting the zero key and
not the letter "O." (On the screen, the zero key has a slash through it.)
Press CR.

The answer comes back −125.6826—but not *quite* so instantaneously.

So far, we've simply proved that the computer can perform like a
calculator. That's no big deal. What'll it do that a calculator can't?

5. Type PRINT "MICHAEL CRICHTON," and press CR. The
machine prints my name. Make it print yours.

6. Now type:

```
FOR X = 1 TO 20 : PRINT TAB (X) : PRINT
"YOUR NAME HERE": NEXT
```

Fill in your name between the quotation marks. When you're sure
the line is typed exactly right, press CR. You should get a staircase of
names. Not bad—although not exactly earth-shattering either. Anyway,
the machine seems to handle words.

7. Now type:

```
SOUND 500,2.0
```

And press CR. Now try:

```
SOUND 1000,2.5
```

Try some other variations on the tone (the first number) and the
duration (the second number). When you're bored with that, turn the
machine off.

For the next part, you will need an IBM DOS disk and a blank disk.

. . .

1. Hold the **IBM DOS** disk in your hand, with the label up and your thumb on the label. Put the disk into drive A (the drive on the left) and close the door.

2. Now turn the computer on. The disk drive will whirr and hum. Eventually the noise will stop and you'll see a message asking you to enter current date and time. Since you don't want a machine ordering you around, press CR twice and the message goes away.

Now you should have a prompt that says > A, followed by the cursor. Press the CAPS LOCK key before continuing.

3. Type **DISKCOPY A: B:** and press CR.
Now you get a message that says:

```
INSERT SOURCE DISK IN DRIVE A
INSERT TARGET DISK IN DRIVE B
STRIKE ANY KEY WHEN READY
```

Put your blank disk in drive B, and strike any key when ready. Now you get a message that reads:

```
COPYING 1 SIDE(S)
```

If the disk has never been used before, it will also say:

```
FORMATTING WHILE COPYING
```

Both drives will beep and whirr for a while now. What the IBM is doing is formatting the blank disk. This means it's arranging the disk to the IBM's particular requirements—rather like putting the company letterhead on a piece of blank stationery. You must format any new disk before you can use it. The IBM is also copying the entire DOS disk onto the new disk.

4. When the noise stops and the light goes out, you get a message:

```
COPY COMPLETE
COPY ANOTHER (Y/N)
```

Type N, and the procedure is done.
Now let's see what's on our new disk. Type B: and press CR. (From here on I'll stop reminding you about CR at the end of a line.) Now you get a prompt that says > B.

Type DIR.

DIR, for DIRectory, is the command to ask what's on the disk. You can ask it at any time. This time, you will see a long list of programs. Let's get rid of them.

Type ERASE *.* (Make sure there are no spaces in "*.*".) The screen will show:

```
ARE YOU SURE (Y/N)?
```

Type Y. It whirrs for a minute, and then it's done. Now type DIR again to see what's happened. You get:

```
FILE NOT FOUND
```

Meaning that there are no files or programs on the disk. But actually this isn't true: you have the operating system on the disk, but it doesn't show in the DIR.

5. Now let's return to drive A. Type A: to put you back in drive A. (If you type DIR, you'll see all those programs again.)

Now type:

```
COPY COMMAND.COM B:
```

When you get the prompt again, type:

```
COPY BASICA.COM B:
```

Now return to drive B, by typing B: . When you now type DIR, you will see that these two files have indeed been transferred to your new disk.

Now we're going to enter a program of our own. Because it'll be a BASIC language program, we first have to enter the BASIC language mode. Type:

```
BASICA
```

Now you get a new prompt: the letters OK and the dash cursor on the line below. This means it's ready for your BASIC program.

Type CLS. This command just clears the screen, but doesn't eliminate memory.

6. Now type the following program exactly, with a CR after each line. Don't worry if you don't understand it.

```
10   FOR X = 1 TO 100
14   A$ = "THIS COMPUTER IS A PUSSYCAT"
20   PRINT USING "&" ; A$ ;
30   NEXT X
100  END
```

Look at the screen. If you've made a mistake in any line (maybe you left out the semicolons in line 20), just retype the line now. The computer will replace the old line with the new one, and arrange your instructions in numerical order before it runs it. To see that happen, type LIST. The program is now listed correctly.

7. Type RUN to run this program. Not bad—but not great.

Type LIST to list the program. You'll see your original five lines. Let's make it more interesting, and make the machine work a little harder.

8. Type the following additional lines:

```
12 COLOR 0,7
40 COLOR 7,0
```

To reassure yourself that the computer has inserted these new lines in the proper place, type LIST again. You'll see:

```
10   FOR X = 1 TO 100
12   COLOR 0,7
14   A$ = "THIS COMPUTER IS A PUSSYCAT"
20   PRINT USING "&";A$;
30   NEXT X
40   COLOR 7,0
100  END
```

RUN the program.

9. Type two more lines:

```
22 COLOR 7,0
24 PRINT "                         " ;
```

You'll want about fifteen spaces between the quotes. Just press the space bar. (The exact number doesn't matter.)

LIST it to see the lines have been put in correctly. Then RUN it. It's getting better, isn't it?

10. LIST it again. You'll see this:

```
10   FOR X = 1 TO 100
12   COLOR 0,7
14   A$ = "THIS COMPUTER IS A PUSSYCAT"
20   PRINT USING "&";A$;
22   COLOR 7,0
24   PRINT "                      ";
30   NEXT X
40   COLOR 7,0
100  END
```

Suppose you like this program and want to save it permanently.

11. Type SAVE "PUSSYCAT. Whenever you SAVE or LOAD a file, you must put the left side in quotation marks.

You'll see the disk-drive light go on; it'll whirr. Your program, called PUSSYCAT, is being SAVEd on the disk. When the red light goes out,

12. Type FILES. You see a new program, PUSSYCAT, has been added to the disk. (It's marked PUSSYCAT.BAS to tell you it's a basic program.) PUSSYCAT is there whenever you want it. But the same program is also still in the machine. Because disk commands such as SAVE or FILES don't alter the computer memory.

13. Type RUN. It still runs.

Type LIST. It still lists, so it's there.

Type FILES

Type PRINT 5 + 5

Type PRINT "DONALD DUCK"

Type FILES again.

Type LIST, to see that all these direct commands did not hurt the program.

This is important: the computer is like a typewriter in an office. That typewriter doesn't care if you stop typing to look up an address in a file cabinet. It doesn't even know you've stopped. In the same way, the computer doesn't know you stopped programming to check the FILES, or to do a little addition on the side. This is very hard to get straight: the disk and the computer memory are separate.

14. Type NEW. That'll get rid of PUSSYCAT.

Now type RUN, and LIST. Nothing happens, because the program was erased from memory.

But the program is still on the disk. Type FILES and you'll see it: PUSSYCAT.BAS.

15. To get the program back in memory, type LOAD "PUSSYCAT and the disk whirrs for a while. When the cursor blinks, meaning the computer is ready, type LIST and RUN. You've got your program back.

16. Type FILES. Notice that PUSSYCAT is still on the disk. Just because you LOADed it into memory, you didn't erase it from the disk. You just made a copy, like a Xerox.

Right now, you have two copies of PUSSYCAT: one in memory, one on the disk.

17. LIST it. You'll see:

```
10   FOR X = 1 TO 100
12   COLOR 0,7
14   A$ = "THIS COMPUTER IS A
     PUSSYCAT"
20   PRINT USING "&";A$;
22   COLOR 7,0
24   PRINT "                    ";
30   NEXT X
40   COLOR 7,0
100  END
```

Now let's make some changes. Type:

```
12 COLOR 16,7
14 A$ = "YOUR NAME CONTROLS THIS PUSSYCAT"
```

But fill in your name in line 14, as in:

```
14 A$ = "DONALD DUCK CONTROLS THIS
   PUSSYCAT";
```

If you LIST it again, you'll see the computer has dutifully made the changes in the correct line numbers.

RUN it.

Depending on how long your name is, it might look better to change the number of spaces in line 24. Anyhow, change the number of spaces, just for fun. Make it much longer or much shorter.

LIST it after you've run it.

Let's say you like this program, too. To save it, type SAVE "PUSYCAT2. (You have to shorten it because the IBM doesn't accept more than 8 letters or numbers for a file name.) Again the disk drive whirrs.

Type FILES. You now see four programs: COMMAND.COM, BASICA.COM, PUSSYCAT.BAS, and PUSYCAT2.BAS.

Turn the machine off.

Now that the machine is off, all programs in the memory are erased. But these programs are still on the disk. Take your own disk out of drive B (the drive on the right) and look at it.

No change—it looks exactly the same as before.

Identify your disk by writing on the label gently with a felt-tip pen. If you don't do that with your disks, you'll get hopelessly confused.

Remove the DOS disk from drive A and put it away. You won't need that disk anymore.

1. Put your own disk back in drive A. Turn the machine on. The drive whirrs, and eventually you get > A and a blinking cursor.

Type DIR.

You see your programs in the catalog. But let's make this your own personalized disk. To do that, we are going to go back into BASIC mode. Type:

```
BASICA.
```

And you will get the OK prompt again.

2. Type NEW. Then type:

```
10 REM OPENING PROGRAM
20 CLS
30 PRINT "THIS IS MY FIRST DISK"
40 PRINT :PRINT
50 FILES
60 END
```

REM stands for REMark. REM means "ignore everything following the REM on this line" to the computer.

3. Now RUN the program. It should clear the screen, and print out the names of the files. If it doesn't, type LIST and check it to make sure it's right. Rewrite any incorrect lines. When it works,

4. Type SAVE "OPENING.

Now type SYSTEM to return to DOS. You will have the $>$A prompt. Now type:

```
COPY CON:AUTOEXEC.BAT
BASICA OPENING
```

Now hit the F6 key, which is one of the gray function keys on the far left of the keyboard, and then CR again. You should get a message that says:

```
1 FILE COPIED
```

5. Turn the machine off.
Turn it back on again. Not bad, huh?

6. Type LIST.

You'll see your OPENING program. The OPENING program will now automatically be loaded in whenever you power up with a disk, or, in computer slang, "boot" the disk.

7. Change line 30 to include your own name. To do this type:

```
30 PRINT "THIS IS DONALD DUCK'S FIRST DISK"
```

Except type your name in place of Donald's. Press RETURN after the line. LIST it to see that the change has been made.

8. RUN it to be sure the program is okay, then type SAVE "OPENING. You've now modified your OPENING and resaved it.

Turn the machine off and take a break. You're doing fine.

Now let's do one numerical problem. Turn the machine back on with your disk in drive A. We're going to convert your height from feet to centimeters. The table in my dictionary says there're 2.54 centimeters to the inch.

1. Type **NEW** and type **CLS** to clear memory and clear the screen. Type the following program:

```
10 REM HEIGHT
20 INPUT "WHAT IS YOUR HEIGHT IN FEET,
   INCHES";F,I
30 C = (F * 12 + I) * 2.54
40 PRINT
50 PRINT "YOUR HEIGHT IS";C;
   "CENTIMETERS"
60 END
```

RUN this program. Enter feet, then a comma, then inches. It works, right? If it doesn't, **LIST** it and check the lines to make sure they're correctly typed in.

Run it a couple of more times, with different heights. You'll find it's a bit neater if you add

```
15 CLS
```

2. Type **SAVE** "HEIGHT. When the disk gets through, turn the machine off.

Take a break. We're going to do just two more programs, but they'll be much more interesting.

1. Boot your disk. (Put the disk in drive A, close the door, and turn IBM on.)

2. Type **NEW**. Type **CLS**.

3. Now type the following:

```
10  REM PYRAMIDS
80  V= 3 : LOCATE V,1
100 W$ = "PYRAMIDS ARE FUN"
110 FOR X = 1 TO LEN (W$)/2
120 LOCATE V, (40 - X)
130 PRINT LEFT$ (W$,X);
```

```
140 PRINT RIGHT$ (W$,X)
145 V = V + 1
150 NEXT X
160 END
```

RUN this, then list the program. (If you're getting tired of typing RUN and LIST, you don't have to do it anymore. Look at your function keys on the left. F2 means RUN. F1 means LIST. So to run, press F2, and to list, press F1 and CR.)

Now add the following lines:

```
20 CLS
100 W$ = "PYRAMID AND THE CORE THE AND
   PYRAMID"
```

Put two spaces between each of the words. Type RUN, or press F2. It looks better now. Add the following lines:

```
30 FOR X = 1 TO 23
40 COLOR 0,7
50 PRINT "++++++++++++++++++++++++++++++++++++
   ++++++++++++++++++++++++++++++++++++++++++++
   ++++++"
60 NEXT X
70 COLOR 7,0
```

There should be about 79 addition signs in line 50. Now RUN this. If you like it,

3. Type SAVE "PYRAMID. Now you have it safely on the disk.

4. I have not told you how the program actually works. But you can still fiddle with it. For example:

Change the quoted words in 100 to something else, and run it. See what happens.

Change line 40 from COLOR 0,7 to COLOR 16,7. Run the program now.

Change the background in line 50 and run it. Make a line of asterisks, or dashes, or just spaces.

Notice you can fool with this program in perfect safety. Even if you screw it up hopelessly, you can always LOAD "PYRAMID from the disk and get back the original program off the disk.

If you stumble upon something that you like, just type SAVE "PYRAMID2 or whatever you want to name it. It's your program, after all. Call it whatever you want.

Turn the machine off. Take the disk out.

If you have a color/graphics adapter, you can jump down to the bottom of the page. Otherwise, let's finish off with two amusing sound programs written by Lisa Faversham:

```
10  REM SCALE
20  SCALE$="CDEFGAB"
30  PLAY"XSCALE$;O5;C"
40  END
```

Make sure there are no spaces in lines 20 and 30, and that in line 30 you have the letter "O," not zero. Run it, and if you like it, SAVE it. Then type NEW, and:

```
10   REM SOUND EFX
20   FOR R = 10 TO 500 STEP 30
30   FOR X = 100 TO 1200 STEP R
40   SOUND X,.05
50   NEXT X
60   FOR X = 1200 TO 100 STEP − R
70   SOUND X,.05
80   NEXT X
90   NEXT R
100  END
```

This time, in lines 40 and 70 it should be a zero and not a letter "O." Run this program and play with it until you drive everybody in the family crazy. (They may not want to let you SAVE it.)

Call it a day.

Turn everything off, put your disk away in its jacket safely. You're done!

If you have a color/graphics adapter, add the following program:

```
10  REM spirals
15  CLS
20  LOCATE 23,2
30  INPUT "angle"; A
```

```
32  CLS
35  IF A = 0 THEN END
40  C = .0174
50  SCREEN 1
60  X1 = 150 : Y1 = 90
70  N = A
80  FOR L = 1 TO 140
85  R = C * A : S = A/N
90  X2 = X1 + S * COS (R)
100 Y2 = Y1 - S * SIN (R)
120 LINE (X1, Y1) - (X2, Y2),1
130 A = A + N : X1 = X2 : Y1 = Y2
140 NEXT L
200 GOTO 20
```

You've now fiddled with numbers, words, and sound. You've learned a bit about using disks. If you decide to go further with programming, you'll find that making the machine do more complex things isn't really harder—it just takes a longer program.

If you want to pursue programming in an orderly fashion, get a good IBM tutorial book. After this session, you'll find a lot of it will be at least slightly familiar to you.

Mystery-Writer Program

The following will undoubtedly prove revolutionary and invaluable for writers everywhere. The program is written for an IBM PC but can be easily modified to run on any machine.

```
10 REM mystery writer helper
20 REM
30 REM 3/82 by mc
40 REM
50 V$=RIGHT$(TIME$,2):V=VAL(V$):
   RANDOMIZE V
60 CLS:PRINT "MYSTERY WRITER'S HELPER":
   PRINT "---------------------"
70 CT=1: REM counter
80 N=22: REM number of answers
```

```
 90   DIM R$(50) : FOR V=1 TO N:READ R$(V):
      NEXT
100   PRINT:PRINT:PRINT "TYPE ANY KEY TO
      GET HELP"
110   A$=INKEY$:IF A$="" THEN 110
120   X=INT(RND*(N+1))
130   PRINT
140   LOCATE 10,1:PRINT R$(X)
150   LOCATE 18,1:PRINT "(M)ORE OR HAD
      (E)NOUGH"
160   LOCATE 19,1: PRINT SPC
170   LOCATE 19,1
180   INPUT A$
190   IF CT=4 THEN 240
200   IF A$<>"M" AND A$<>"m" AND  A$<>"E"
      AND A$<>"e" THEN A$="m"
210   IF A$="M" OR A$="m" THEN CT=CT+1:
      GOTO 230
220   IF A$="E" OR A$="e" GOTO 250
230   LOCATE 10,1:PRINT SPC(40): GOTO 120
240   LOCATE 10,1: COLOR 0,7:PRINT"
      YOU WANT TOO MUCH HELP!!!        ":
      COLOR 7,0
250   LOCATE 23,1:END
260   REM
270   REM----data statements-----
280   REM
290   DATA you get knocked out, you go
      somewhere else
300   DATA you find a dead man, you find a
      dead woman
310   DATA you find a buxom blonde,
      someone searched the place
320   DATA a crooked cop warns you, you
      are arrested
330   DATA you find a gun, you find a
      knife
340   DATA you find a frayed rope, a
      bullet whizzes past your ear!!
350   DATA you are almost run over, you
      are being followed
360   DATA you smell familiar perfume, the
      telephone rings
370   DATA there is a knock at the door,
      you hear footsteps behind you
```

```
380 DATA you hear a gunshot, you hear a
    scream
390 DATA you are not alone, forget this
    story—it stinks!
```

Non-Rational Programs

Computers can be used for almost anything. I'm interested in the I Ching, an ancient Chinese method of telling the future. My I CHING program, with comments, an explanation of how the program works, and suggestions for modifications, originally appeared in *Creative Computing,* March, 1983. The version presented here has been modified to make it more easily adapted to other machines.

How the I Ching works—and whether it works at all—is an interesting speculation. The Chinese text is wise in any case. I find the I Ching valuable, although I have no interest in astrology and other divination techniques.

The method by which the I Ching arrives at an answer is quite complicated. It's natural to wonder whether the method has real power, or whether we will derive meaning from any reasonably cryptic answer to our questions. To get a sense of the extent to which we tend to supply our own meanings, I wrote SOOTHSAYER.

SOOTHSAYER is extremely simple, as simple as MYSTERY WRITER. The program selects an answer at random to your question, and thus it might be thought of as a control for the I Ching. This depends on your concept of chance and random events. If you have any sympathy for ideas such as Jung's notion of synchronicity, you will tend to see both the I CHING and SOOTHSAYER as subject to unexplained controlling influences of a similar sort. That would make SOOTHSAYER merely a not very wise version of the I CHING. Similarly, if you think this Eastern mysticism is all mumbo jumbo, then both programs will be perceived as mumbo jumbo in the same way.

Yet from one standpoint it seems to me that these programs have indisputable value. We all have unconscious thoughts that influence our perceptions and behavior to a far greater degree than we care to admit. It seems worthwhile to bring these influences to conscious awareness by any means possible. For that reason alone, the programs—and our reactions to them—are worth our attention.

```
10    REM  I CHING
11    REM
13    REM  --------------------------
14    REM   THIS PROGRAM THROWS &
16    REM   LOOKS UP HEXAGRAMS
18    REM   AND ALSO GENERATES
19    REM   SECONDARY AND NUCLEAR
20    REM   HEXAGRAMS
22    REM  ------------------------
23    REM
24    REM   COMPLETED 9/23/82
26    REM   BY MICHAEL CRICHTON
28    REM
50    REM ******INITIALIZATION******
51    REM
52    KEY OFF
53    REM T=LOOKUP TABLE, R$=RESPONSES
55    DIM T(8,8): FOR V=1 TO 8: FOR H=1 TO
      8: READ T(V,H):NEXT H,V
56    DIM R$(64): FOR V=1 TO 64: READ R$(V):
      NEXT V
99    REM
100   REM *****FIRST OPTIONS*****
110   REM
120   CLS
130   LOCATE 8,31: COLOR 0,7: PRINT " I
      CHING PROGRAM  ": COLOR 7,0: LOCATE
      11,39: PRINT "BY": LOCATE 14,33:
      PRINT "MICHAEL CRICHTON"
140   LOCATE 22,18:PRINT"(I)NSTRUCTIONS,
      (C)OINS, OR (M)ACHINE INPUT  ";:
      INPUT A$
150   IF A$="I" OR A$="i" GOTO 6000:REM
      INSTR
160   IF A$="C" OR A$="c" GOTO 200:REM
      COINS
170   IF A$="M" OR A$="m" GOTO 300: REM
      MACHINE INPUT
180   REM
200   REM *****COIN INPUT*****
205   REM
210   CLS:PS=18
220   LOCATE 8,1: PRINT "TOSS COINS SIX
      TIMES..."
230   FOR I=1 TO 6
```

```
240 LOCATE PS,1: INPUT L(I)
250 IF L(I)<6 OR L(I)>9 THEN LOCATE PS,1:
    PRINT"      VALUE UNACCEPTABLE":GOTO
    240
270 PS=PS-1: NEXT I
280 GOTO 600
290 REM
300 REM *****MACHINE INPUT*****
310 REM
311 CLS: PS=18
320 LOCATE 8,1:PRINT "PRESS KEYBOARD SIX
    TIMES..."
330 FOR I=1 TO 6
340 CH=INT(RND(1) * 100)
345 REM FIRST COIN
350 X= INT(RND(1)*CH)
360 IF X/2=INT(X/2) THEN C1=2: GOTO 380
370 C1=3
380 REM NEXT COIN
390 X=INT(RND(1)*CH)
400 IF X/2=INT(X/2) THEN C2=2: GOTO 420
410 C2=3
420 REM NEXT COIN
430 X=INT(RND(1) * CH)
440 IF X/2=INT(X/2) THEN C3=2: GOTO 485
450 C3=3
470 REM
480 REM KEYBOARD PRESSED???
485 REM
490 A$=INKEY$: IF A$="" THEN 340
500 GOTO 520
510 REM
520 REM KEYBOARD WAS PRESSED
525 REM
530 L(I)=C1+C2+C3: LOCATE PS,1: PRINT
    L(I)
550 PS=PS-1: NEXT I
555 BEEP:REM WARNING BEEP
560 REM
600 REM *****BEGIN PROCESSING*****
610 REM
620 LOCATE 12,1: PRINT "HEXAGRAM
    COMPLETED": FOR DL=1 TO 500:NEXT
630 CLS
```

```
640 REM
650 PS=20
660 FOR I=1 TO 6
670 L=L(I):LOCATE PS,15: GOSUB 2000
675 PS=PS-3
680 NEXT I
690 LOCATE 23,1
699 REM
700 REM ****READ ANSWER****
705 REM
710 L1$=STR$(L(1)): L2$=STR$(L(2)): L3$=
    STR$(L(3)):L4$=STR$(L(4)):L5$=
    STR$(L(5)): L6$=STR$(L(6))
730 LT$=L1$+L2$+L3$: UT$=L4$+L5$+L6$:REM:
    UPPER/LOWER TRIGRAMS
740 T1$=LT$: GOSUB 2200: GOSUB 3000
750 LT=TM
760 T1$=UT$: GOSUB 2200: GOSUB 3000
770 UT=TM
780 H1=T(LT,UT): REM primary hexagram
    val
790 LOCATE   22,1: PRINT " # " ;H1;
    "    "; R$(H1)
800 FOR DL=1 TO 500: NEXT DL
810 LOCATE 24,1: PRINT " LINES ARE:   ";
    L1$;"-";L2$;"-";L3$;"-";L4$;"-";L5$;
    "-";L6$;"      ";:INPUT A$
820 REM ****OTHER TRIGRAMS****
830 REM SECONDARY TRIGRAM
840 T2$=LT$: GOSUB 2300: GOSUB 3000: LT=
    TM
850 T2$=UT$: GOSUB 2300: GOSUB 3000: UT=
    TM
860 H2=T(LT,UT): REM H2=2NDARY HEXAGRAM
    VAL
870 REM FIRST NUCLEAR
880 LN$=L2$+L3$+L4$: UN$=L3$+L4$+L5$
890 T1$=LN$: GOSUB 2200: GOSUB 3000: LN=
    TM
900 T1$=UN$: GOSUB 2200: GOSUB 3000: UN=
    TM
910 N1=T(LN,UN): REM NUCLEAR 1 HEX VAL
920 REM SECOND NUCLEAR
```

```
930  T2$=LN$: GOSUB 2300: GOSUB 3000: LN=
     TM
940  T2$=UN$: GOSUB 2300: GOSUB 3000: UN=
     TM
950  N2=T(LN,UN):REM NUCLEAR 2 HEX VAL
960  REM
1245 REM ****SUMMARY PAGE****
1246 REM
1250 CLS
1285 OPEN "SCRN:" FOR OUTPUT AS #1
1290 FLAG=0
1292 PRINT #1,"CASTING WAS: ";L1$;"-";
     L2$;"-";L3$;"-";L4$;"-";L5$;"-";L6$
1294 PRINT #1,"--------------------------
     --------------"
1295 PRINT #1,"PRIMARY HEXAGRAM-":PRINT
     #1," "
1297 PRINT #1,TAB(6): PRINT #1, H1;"   ";
     R$(H1):PRINT #1," "
1300 PRINT #1,"SECONDARY HEXAGRAM-":
     PRINT #1," "
1310 PRINT #1,TAB(6):PRINT #1,H2;"   ";
     R$(H2):PRINT #1," "
1320 PRINT #1,"FIRST NUCLEAR-": PRINT
     #1," "
1330 PRINT #1,TAB(6):PRINT #1,N1;"   ";
     R$(N1):PRINT #1," "
1340 PRINT #1,"SECOND NUCLEAR-": PRINT
     #1," "
1350 PRINT #1,TAB(6): PRINT #1,N2;"   ";
     R$(N2):PRINT #1," "
1352 CLOSE #1
1355 IF FLAG=1 THEN 1379
1360 PRINT:PRINT:PRINT "DO YOU WANT A
     PRINTOUT (Y/N)";:INPUT A$
1361 LOCATE 21,1:PRINT SPC(40)
1363 IF A$="N" OR A$="n" GOTO 1379
1364 LOCATE 21,1: INPUT "TODAY'S DATE
     (MM/DD/YY)";D$
1365 LOCATE 21,1: PRINT SPC(50)
1367 LOCATE 21,1: PRINT "WHAT WAS YOUR
     QUESTION": INPUT Q$:LPRINT D$:
     LPRINT Q$
1368 LOCATE 22,1: PRINT SPC(40)
```

```
1369 OPEN "LPT1:" FOR OUTPUT AS #1
1370 FLAG=1
1372 GOTO 1292
1379 KEY ON: END
1380 REM
1998 REM *****START SUBROUTINES*****
1999 REM
2000 REM *****DRAW GRAPHIC*****
2005 REM
2008 COLOR 0,7
2010 IF L=6 THEN PRINT SPC(20);:COLOR
     7,0:PRINT SPC(10);:COLOR 0,7:PRINT
     SPC(20):COLOR 7,0: RETURN
2020 IF L=7 THEN PRINT SPC(50):COLOR 7,0:
     RETURN
2030 IF L=8 THEN PRINT SPC(20);:COLOR
     7,0:PRINT SPC(10);:COLOR 0,7:PRINT
     SPC(20):COLOR 7,0: RETURN
2040 IF L=9 THEN PRINT SPC(50):COLOR 7,0:
     RETURN
2050 REM
2100 REM *****2NDARY HEX CONVERSION*****
2105 REM
2110 IF L=6 THEN L=7: RETURN
2120 IF L=9 THEN L=8: RETURN
2130 REM
2200 REM ****CONVERT TRIGRAM #'S FOR
     LOOKUP****
2205 REM
2210 S$="":X$="":REM NULL
2220 FOR N=1 TO LEN(T1$)
2230 X$=MID$(T1$,N,1)
2240 IF X$="6" THEN X$="8"
2250 IF X$="9" THEN X$="7"
2260 S$=S$+X$: NEXT N
2270 T1$=S$:RETURN
2280 REM
2300 REM ****CONVERT OTHER TRIGRAMS****
2305 REM
2310 S$="":X$="":REM NULL
2320 FOR N=1 TO LEN(T2$)
2330 X$=MID$(T2$,N,1)
2340 IF X$="6" THEN X$="7"
```

```
2350 IF X$="9" THEN X$="8"
2360 S$=S$+X$:NEXT N
2370 T1$=S$: RETURN
2380 REM
3000 REM ****CONVERT 1-8****
3005 REM
3010 TM=VAL(T1$)
3020 IF TM=777 THEN TM=1: GOTO 3100
3030 IF TM=788 THEN TM=2: GOTO 3100
3040 IF TM=878 THEN TM=3: GOTO 3100
3050 IF TM=887 THEN TM=4: GOTO 3100
3060 IF TM=888 THEN TM=5: GOTO 3100
3070 IF TM=877 THEN TM=6: GOTO 3100
3080 IF TM=787 THEN TM=7: GOTO 3100
3090 IF TM=778 THEN TM=8: GOTO 3100
3100 RETURN
3110 REM
3500 REM ****LOOKUP TABLE DATA****
3510 REM
3520 DATA 1,34,5,26,11,9,14,43
3530 DATA 25,51,3,27,24,42,21,17
3540 DATA 60,40,29,4,7,59,64,47
3550 DATA 33,62,39,52,15,53,56,31
3560 DATA 12,16,8,23,2,20,35,45
3570 DATA 44,32,48,18,46,57,50,28
3580 DATA 13,55,63,22,36,37,30,49
3590 DATA 10,54,60,41,19,61,38,58
3595 REM
4000 REM ****RESPONSE DATA****
4010 REM
4020 DATA THE CREATIVE
4030 DATA THE RECEPTIVE
4040 DATA DIFFICULT BEGINNINGS
4050 DATA YOUTHFUL FOLLY (INEXPERIENCE)
4060 DATA CALCULATED WAITING
4070 DATA CONFLICT
4080 DATA THE ARMY
4090 DATA HOLDING TOGETHER
4100 DATA THE TAMING POWER OF THE SMALL
4110 DATA RESTRAINED CONDUCT (TREADING)
4120 DATA PEACE
4130 DATA STAGNATION
4140 DATA FELLOWSHIP WITH MEN
```

```
4150 DATA POSSESSION IN GREAT MEASURE
4160 DATA MODESTY (MODERATION)
4170 DATA ENTHUSIASM
4180 DATA FOLLOWING
4190 DATA WORK AT WHAT HAS BEEN SPOILED
4200 DATA APPROACH
4210 DATA CONTEMPLATION
4220 DATA BITING THROUGH
4230 DATA GRACE
4240 DATA DETERIORATION (SPLITTING
     APART)
4250 DATA RETURN
4260 DATA INNOCENCE
4270 DATA THE TAMING POWER OF THE GREAT
4280 DATA NOURISHMENT
4290 DATA PREPONDERANCE OF THE GREAT
4300 DATA THE ABYSMAL (DANGER)
4310 DATA THE CLINGING
4320 DATA ATTRACTION
4330 DATA ENDURING
4340 DATA RETREAT
4350 DATA THE POWER OF THE GREAT
4360 DATA PROGRESS
4370 DATA DARKENING OF THE LIGHT
4380 DATA THE FAMILY
4390 DATA OPPOSITION
4400 DATA OBSTRUCTION
4410 DATA DELIVERANCE (LIBERATION)
4420 DATA DECREASE
4430 DATA INCREASE
4440 DATA RESOLUTION
4450 DATA COMING TO MEET (TEMPTATION)
4460 DATA GATHERING TOGETHER
4470 DATA PUSHING UPWARD
4480 DATA OPPRESSION
4490 DATA THE SOURCE (THE WELL)
4500 DATA REVOLUTION
4510 DATA THE CALDRON
4520 DATA AROUSING (SHOCK)
4530 DATA KEEPING STILL
4540 DATA DEVELOPMENT
4550 DATA THE MARRYING MAIDEN
4560 DATA ABUNDANCE
4570 DATA TRAVELLING
4580 DATA GENTLE INFLUENCE
```

```
4590 DATA JOY
4600 DATA DISPERSION
4610 DATA LIMITATIONS
4620 DATA INNER TRUTH
4630 DATA PREPONDERANCE OF THE SMALL
4640 DATA AFTER COMPLETION
4650 DATA BEFORE COMPLETION
4660 :
4670 :
6000 REM ****INSTRUCTIONS****
6010 CLS
6020 PRINT"THE I CHING IS AN ANCIENT
     CHINESE METHOD OF DIVINATION.  BY
     REPEATEDLY"
6030 PRINT"THROWING STICKS OR COINS, A
     SIX-LINE FIGURE, OR HEXAGRAM, IS
     CREATED."
6035 PRINT
6040 PRINT"THIS HEXAGRAM IS INTERPRETED
     BY CONSULTING A METAPHORICAL TEXT."
6050 PRINT
6060 PRINT"FURTHER INFORMATION CAN BE
     OBTAINED BY DERIVING A SECONDARY
     HEXAGRAM,"
6070 PRINT"AND TWO SO-CALLED 'NUCLEAR
     HEXAGRAMS'."
6075 PRINT
6080 PRINT "THIS PROGRAM PROVIDES THE
     HEXAGRAM NAMES ONLY. FOR FURTHER
     INTER-"
6085 PRINT "PRETATION, USER SHOULD
     OBTAIN A GOOD I CHING TEXT, SUCH AS
     THE CLASSIC"
6087 PRINT "TRANSLATION BY RICHARD
     WILHELM (PRINCETON UNIVERSITY
     PRESS)."
6090 GOSUB 8000
6100 CLS:PRINT SPC(30):PRINT "CASTING
     THE I CHING"
6110 PRINT: PRINT SPC(33): COLOR 0,7:
     PRINT" WITH COINS ": COLOR 7,0
6120 PRINT
6130 PRINT "USE THREE SIMILAR COINS SUCH
     AS PENNIES. ASSIGN ONE FACE THE
     VALUE OF 3 AND THE OTHER FACE THE
     VALUE OF 2."
```

```
6133 PRINT
6135 PRINT "THINK ON YOUR QUESTION AS
     YOU CAST THE COINS SIX TIMES."
6140 PRINT
6150 PRINT "AFTER EACH THROW, SUM THE
     THREE FACES, TO GET A VALUE FROM 6
     TO 9. ENTER THIS"
6155 PRINT "VALUE INTO THE COMPUTER."
6160 PRINT:PRINT:PRINT SPC(33):COLOR 0,7:
     PRINT " BY COMPUTER ": COLOR 7,0:
     PRINT
6170 PRINT
6180 PRINT "THE COMPUTER WILL SIMULATE
     COIN TOSSES IF YOU PRESS ANY KEY
     SIX TIMES."
6190 GOSUB 8000
6200 CLS: PRINT "INTERPRETING THE I
     CHING":PRINT:PRINT
6210 PRINT "THE COMPUTER FIRST GENERATES
     THE PRIMARY HEXAGRAM.":PRINT
6220 PRINT: PRINT
6230 PRINT "IT WILL THEN ADD THE
     HEXAGRAM NAME, AND THE LINE VALUES
     READING FROM"
6235 PRINT "BOTTOM TO TOP":PRINT
6240 PRINT
6290 PRINT "<RETURN> WILL SUMMARIZE THE
     DATA ON ALL FOUR HEXAGRAMS, AND
     PROVIDE A PRINTOUT"
6295 PRINT "OPTION"
6300 GOTO 140
6310 REM
7997 REM
7998 REM ***PAUSE***
7999 REM
8000 LOCATE 24,1: PRINT "PRESS ANY KEY
     TO CONTINUE";: INPUT A$: RETURN
```

```
10    REM    SOOTHSAYER
20    REM
30    REM  ------------------
40    REM
50    REM   COMPLETED 10/23/82
60    REM   BY MICHAEL CRICHTON
70    REM
80    REM
90    REM   ***** INITIALIZATION *****
100  KEY OFF
110  DIM R$(64):FOR V=1 TO 64:READ R$(V):
     NEXT V
120  V$=RIGHT$(TIME$,2):V=VAL(V$):
     RANDOMIZE V
130  CLS
140  LOCATE 8,30
150  COLOR 0,7:PRINT "    SOOTHSAYER    ":
     COLOR 7,0
160  LOCATE 11,40: PRINT "BY": LOCATE
     14,32: PRINT "MICHAEL CRICHTON"
170  LOCATE 22,1:PRINT "PRESS ANY KEY TO
     BEGIN";:INPUT A$
180  REM
190  REM ***** BEGIN INPUT *****
200  REM
210  CLS:LOCATE 8,1: PRINT "WHAT IS YOUR
     QUESTION?"
220  LOCATE 10,1: INPUT Q$
230  IF LEN(Q$)<8 THEN LOCATE 14,1:
     PRINT"SORRY, DIDN'T HEAR THAT...":
     GOTO 290
240  REM
250  REM ***** MAKE RESPONSE *****
260  REM
270  V=INT(RND    *(64+1))
280  LOCATE 14,1:PRINT R$(V)
290  LOCATE 22,1:PRINT "DO YOU WISH TO
     ASK ANOTHER QUESTION (Y/N)?": INPUT
     A$
300  IF A$="N" OR A$ = "n" THEN 330
310  GOTO 210
320  REM ***** ENDING *****
330  CLS
340  LOCATE 8,1: PRINT "THE CONSULTATION
     IS AT AN END.": PRINT: PRINT "LIVE
```

```
            AND  PROSPER  IN  THE  KNOWLEDGE":
            PRINT"THAT  MY  ANSWERS  ARE  TOTALLY
            RANDOM"
350  KEY  ON
360  PRINT:PRINT:PRINT:PRINT:PRINT:PRINT:
            PRINT:END
370  REM  ****DATA  ENTRIES****
380  DATA  ONE  CAN  KNOW  GOOD  ONLY  BECAUSE
            THERE  IS  EVIL
390  DATA  THE  MIND  IS  FULL  OF  QUESTIONS
            BUT  THE  HEART  KNOWS  ALL
400  DATA  NOT  COLLECTING  TREASURES
            PREVENTS  STEALING
410  DATA  BE  STILL
420  DATA  HOLD  FAST  TO  THE  CENTER
430  DATA  EASY  COME  EASY  GO
440  DATA  HEAVEN  AND  HELL  ARE  BOTH  WITHIN
450  DATA  A  GREAT  TAILOR  CUTS  LITTLE
460  DATA  PRACTICE  RESTRAINT
470  DATA  TAKE  CARE  OF  ALL  THINGS  AND
            ABANDON  NOTHING
480  DATA  TO  BE  RESTLESS  IS  TO  LOSE  ONE'S
            CONTROL
490  DATA  HE  WHO  DOES  NOT  TRUST  ENOUGH
            WILL  NOT  BE  TRUSTED
500  DATA  RETIRE  WHEN  THE  WORK  IS  DONE
510  DATA  THROUGH  SELFLESS  ACTION  YOU
            WILL  ATTAIN  FULFILLMENT
520  DATA  ACCEPT  MISFORTUNE  AS  THE  HUMAN
            CONDITION
530  DATA  EMPTY  YOURSELF  OF  ALL  DESIRES
540  DATA  GIVE  UP  LEARNING  AND  PUT  AN  END
            TO  YOUR  TROUBLES
550  DATA  UNDERSTANDING  IS  THE  BOOBY
            PRIZE
560  DATA  WE  SEE  THE  WORLD  AS  WE  KNOW  IT
            TO  BE
570  DATA  HE  THAT  CAN  HAVE  PATIENCE  CAN
            HAVE  EVERYTHING
580  DATA  HE  WHO  MAKES  A  SHOW  IS  NOT  THE
            ENLIGHTENED
590  DATA  ONE  CAN  ALWAYS  DEPEND  ON  THE
            KINDNESS  OF  STRANGERS
600  DATA  PRIDE  GOETH  BEFORE  A  FALL
```

```
610 DATA ALL THAT YOU SEEK LIES WITHIN
    YOURSELF
620 DATA WEAPONS ARE NOT THE TOOLS OF
    THE WISE
630 DATA HE WHO KNOWS HE HAS ENOUGH IS
    RICH
640 DATA ROLL WITH THE PUNCHES
650 DATA CHANGE COMES WITH STILLNESS
660 DATA INACTION IS A FORM OF ACTION
670 DATA SEE WHAT IS REAL AND NOT WHAT
    IS APPARENT
680 DATA TOO MUCH SUCCESS IS NOT AN
    ADVANTAGE
690 DATA AS YOU LIVE SO SHALL YOU DIE
700 DATA THE PAST IS THE FATHER OF THE
    FUTURE
710 DATA A CONTENTED MAN IS NEVER
    DISAPPOINTED
720 DATA GREAT INTELLIGENCE SOMETIMES
    SEEMS STUPID
730 DATA THERE ARE NO INNOCENT VICTIMS
740 DATA DISAPPOINTMENT SPRINGS FROM
    DESIRE
750 DATA KEEP YOUR MOUTH SHUT AND YOU
    WILL LEARN PEACE
760 DATA BE SIMPLE AND BE FREE
770 DATA HAPPINESS SPRINGS FROM MISERY
    AND MISERY FROM HAPPINESS. IT IS
    ALWAYS SO
780 DATA HOWEVER GOOD OR BAD IT WILL
    SOON CHANGE
790 DATA WHY DOES THE BLIND MAN'S WIFE
    PAINT HER FACE
800 DATA YOU CAN BE TOO CLEVER FOR YOUR
    OWN GOOD
810 DATA BLISS FOLLOWS DETACHMENT FROM
    WORLDLY DESIRES
820 DATA YOU WORRY ABOUT TRIVIAL MATTERS
830 DATA LIFE IS HARD
840 DATA YOU CAN'T GET ENOUGH OF WHAT
    YOU DON'T NEED
850 DATA HOW MANY PSYCHIATRISTS DOES IT
    TAKE TO CHANGE A LIGHTBULB? ONE--BUT
```

```
          THE LIGHTBULB HAS TO WANT TO CHANGE
 860      DATA ASK YOURSELF HOW YOU HAVE
          GOTTEN INTO THIS STATE
 870      DATA MEDITATE ON FREEDOM FROM CARE
 880      DATA WHEN IN DOUBT THROW IT OUT
 890      DATA SEE THE GOOD IN ALL THINGS
 900      DATA YOU KNOW YOUR QUESTIONS ARE
          EXTREMELY IRRITATING. WHY DON'T YOU
          PULL YOURSELF TOGETHER AND DEAL WITH
          YOUR OWN PROBLEMS?
 910      DATA MAN DOES NOT LIVE BY BREAD
          ALONE
 920      DATA MOST PEOPLE FIND WHAT THEY ARE
          LOOKING FOR--THAT'S THE PROBLEM
 930      DATA MOVE SLOWLY AND SEE
 940      DATA RISK ALL AND GAIN EVERYTHING
 950      DATA ASK HOW YOU HAVE CONTRIBUTED TO
          OR CAUSED THIS SITUATION
 960      DATA LIFE IS A FATAL DISEASE. NO ONE
          SURVIVES IT
 970      DATA LIVE IN THE MOMENT
 980      DATA SEE YOUR WAKING HOURS AS A
          DREAM
 990      DATA YOU ALREADY KNOW THE ANSWER
1000      DATA THE RIVER RUNS FULL IN THE
          SPRING AND DRY IN THE FALL
1010      DATA ALL THINGS END IN THEIR OWN
          TIME
1020      DATA FORTUNE AND MISFORTUNE ARE
          FACES ON THE SAME COIN
```

GROUCHY GLOSSARY

Algorithm. A method for doing something.

Analog. As opposed to digital. For example, representations of numerical values by variations in electrical current, such as a meter with a needle.

Application. Not how you get a job, but what job you set for the computer.

Backup. Copies of data on a storage medium such as floppy disks.

BASIC. Beginners' All-purpose Symbolic Instruction Code. A computer language designed by John Kemeny and Thomas Kurtz of Dartmouth.

Bit. A single switch inside a computer.

Bomb. Computer or program failure. Also, a programmed instruction intended to make the computer fail, as a form of sabotage.

Boot. To turn power up in a system. Generally, to put a disk in the machine and turn the machine on.

Buffer. A special temporary memory for holding data between two areas, such as between the computer memory and the disk or the printer.

Bug. An error that crashes the program.

Bulletproof. Programming routines so well constructed that the user cannot screw them up.

Byte. The unit of information storage in the computer, equivalent to one character of text. Generally comprised of eight bits.

COBOL. Common Business-Oriented Language. Exactly what it says, a programming language for business, developed in the early 1960s.

Code. Programmed instructions to the computer. Source code is the language the program was written in. Object code is the machine language the program is translated into.

Column. The number of characters on the monitor screen.

Compiler. A program that translates high-level language into machine code.

Crash. Computer or program failure.

Data. Information.

Data base. Information fed into the machine, the basis for making decisions or calculations.

Dedicated. A single-purpose machine. Formerly, an electrical line required for a single purpose.

Density. A measure of the closeness that data can be put onto a disk.

Disk. A recording medium for computers, similar to audiotape.

Documentation. Notes and instructions that accompany a machine or program.

Down. Describing a computer that is not working; i.e., the machine is down. Not applied to programs.

Dump. This term refers to evacuating the contents of some part of the machine—a portion of memory, a part of the disk—to the screen or printer. I dislike "dump" but can think of no substitute.

Enhancement. Fancy talk for making something the way it should have been in the first place.

EPROM. Eraseable Programmable Read-Only Memory. A chip that can be programmed, and reprogrammed, at will.

Execution. Of a program, not you. Making it run on the computer.

File. A collected group of records.

Forth. A programming language.

FORTRAN. FORmula TRANslation, a scientific and engineering language.

GIGO. Garbage in, garbage out. A great truth.

Hardware. Nuts-and-bolts equipment.

Input. Whatever is put into the computer.

Interface. The junction of a computer and something else, such as a printer, a telephone line, or a sensing device in the real world. In wider usage, the border of any two things imaginable, such as "the speaker-listener interface." Such ways of speaking generally reflect a spurious attempt to make what is said seem more important, or at least more scientific, than it is.

Kilobyte. One thousand bytes of information, abbreviated K or sometimes KB.

Megabyte. One million bytes of information, abbreviated M, or sometimes MB.

Memory. The storage capacity of a computer. Divided into RAM, Random Access Memory, and ROM, Read-Only Memory. User memory is RAM.

Mode. The method of operating. For example, there are two execution modes, immediate and deferred.

Monitor. A video screen for displaying computer input and output.

Operating system. The internal programs that govern the operation of the computer. Many different computers can run "under" certain popular operating systems, such as CP/M (Control Processor/Microcomputer).

Output. Information transmitted from the computer to an external device such as a printer. In common usage, it has the sense of productivity, which is not correct for a computer. Often applied to people in the sense of productivity.

Packing. Compression of digital data for efficient storage.

Pascal. A high-level language for beginners. Named for Blaise Pascal, a seventeenth-century mathematician. There is no agreement whether this language should be printed upper or lower case, or both.

Program. A sequence of instructions to direct a computer.

PROM. Programmable Read-Only Memory. Computer chips that can be imprinted with fixed programs by the user.

RAM. Random Access Memory. Computer chips available to the users for temporary storage of information. RAM is generally measured in kilobytes (K) or megabytes (M). Information in RAM is held only as long as power is maintained.

Read. To get data from a disk or other storage device.

Retrofit. To fix up later. The engineering sound of this one disguises the true meaning, generally that somebody goofed.

ROM. Read-Only Memory. Computer chips with fixed instructions on them for the computer.

Software. Programs.

Systems. A buzzword. When a skyscraper, a weapon, a town, a doctor's office, a kitchen, and a nuclear family are all systems, it's time to ask what isn't.

Up. Said when a computer is working; i.e., the computer is up.

VLSI. Very Large Scale Integrated microchip. A biggie.

Write. To store data on a disk or other medium.

BIBLIOGRAPHY

A short selection of recent references

Computers Generally

Bernstein, Jeremy. "Marvin Minsky and Artificial Intelligence." *The New Yorker* 57 (December 14, 1981): 50–52+.
A physicist's profile of a pioneering AI researcher; warm, readable, and informative.

Dreyfus, Hubert L. *What Computers Can't Do: A Critique of Artificial Reason.* Rev. ed. New York: Harper & Row, 1979.
A philosopher's scrutiny of AI. Highly critical of the field, and influential among AI researchers. Difficult reading.

Evans, Christopher. *The Micro Millennium.* New York: Viking, 1979.
A concise history of microprocessors by an enthusiast.

Fishman, Katherine Davis. *The Computer Establishment.* New York: Harper & Row, 1981.
Naturally focused on IBM; a good overview of the computer business and how it grew.

Ginzberg, Eli. "The Mechanization of Work." *Scientific American* 247 (September, 1982): 66–76.
The entire issue of this magazine is devoted to this subject, and the articles are uniformly good.

Hansen, Dirk. *The New Alchemists, Silicon Valley and the Microelectronics Revolution.* Boston: Little, Brown, 1982.
More informal history of microchip manufacture and where it may be leading us.

Hofstader, Douglas R. *Godel, Escher, and Bach: An Eternal Golden Braid.* New York: Basic Books, 1979.
Written by a computer scientist, this is a playful and fascinating book. While not directly discussing computers, it tells you an awful lot about them.

Kidder, Tracy. *The Soul of a New Machine.* Boston: Atlantic–Little, Brown, 1981.
How Data General built a 32-bit minicomputer; a case history of life in the computer industry. A justly praised book.

Weizenbaum, Joseph. *Computer Power and Human Reason: From Judgment to Calculation.* San Francisco: W. H. Freeman, 1976.
An assessment of what computers can and can't do by the author of ELIZA. A book many years ahead of its time and widely misunderstood.

Buying Computers

Anonymous. "Home Computers: A Guide for Bewildered Buyers." *Changing Times* 36 (August, 1982): 24–28.
A useful, if superficial, summary of twelve popular small computers. Not technical.

Fawcette, James. "Ada Tackles Software Bottleneck." *High Technology* 3 (February, 1983): 49–54.
A discussion of Ada, and of programming languages in general.

Lu, Cary. "Microcomputers: The Second Wave." *High Technology* 2 (September–October, 1982): 36–52.
Good discussion of 16-bit computers. Informative about computer development generally, as well as summarizing the features of twenty new machines.

————. "Will There Ever be an Efficient Keyboard?" *High Technology* 3 (January, 1983): 22–23.
Amusing discussion of keyboards and future possibilities.

Manus, Steven, and Scriven, Michael. *How to Buy a Word Processor.* An Alfred Handy Guide. Sherman Oaks, Calif.: Alfred Publishing Co., 1982.
Clear, inexpensive, covers the subject tightly. Discusses brand names.

McWilliams, Peter. *The Personal Computer Book.* New York: Ballantine Books / Prelude Press, 1982.

————. *The Word Processing Book: A Short Course in Computer Literacy.* New York: Ballantine Books / Prelude Press, 1982.
Informal, amusing guides that discuss brand names. Prejudiced against simpler, smaller computers, but open about it.

Shrum, Carlton. *How to Buy a Personal Computer.* An Alfred Handy Guide. Sherman Oaks, Calif.: Alfred Publishing Co., 1982.
Inexpensive, clear, comprehensive. Discusses brand names.

Toong, Hoo-Min, and Gupta, Amar. "The Computer Age Gets Personal." *Technology Review* 86 (January, 1983): 26–37.
A straightforward overview.

Using Computers

There are how-to books written for specific computers, and if you own a popular machine, you will be happiest choosing one. Some general books are worth mentioning:

Anonymous. *International Microcomputer Dictionary.* Berkeley: Sybex, 1981.
A pretty good dictionary with translations of technical terms into six languages.

Dwyer, Thomas, and Critchfield, Margot. *Basic and the Personal Computer.* Reading, Mass.: Addison-Wesley, 1978.
A good course of BASIC in eight hour-long lessons. Not written for any particular computer. Unclear on certain subjects, such as arrays, but solid overall.

Mayer, JoAnne Coffman, with Sippl, Charles J. *The Essential Computer Dictionary and Speller for Secretaries, Managers, and Office Personnel.* Englewood Cliffs, N.J.: Prentice-Hall, 1980.
A good dictionary.

Nevison, John M. *The Little Book of BASIC Style: How to Write a Program You Can Read.* Reading, Mass.: Addison-Wesley, 1978.
A tight, readable, clear style book written by someone who is not a computer Calvinist. A wonderful book.

A Note on the Type

The text of this book was set via computer-driven cathode-ray tube in a face called Times Roman, designed by Stanley Morison for The Times (London), and first introduced by that newspaper in 1932.

Among typographers and designers of the twentieth century, Stanley Morison has been a strong forming influence, as typographical advisor to the English Monotype Corporation, as a director of two distinguished English publishing houses, and as a writer of sensibility, erudition, and keen practical sense.

Composed, printed, and bound by The Haddon Craftsmen, Inc., Scranton, Pennsylvania